liberating
CHRIST

EXPLORING THE CHRISTOLOGIES
OF CONTEMPORARY LIBERATION
MOVEMENTS

liberating CHRIST

Lisa Isherwood

The Pilgrim Press
Cleveland, Ohio

The Pilgrim Press, Cleveland, Ohio 44115
© 1999 by Lisa Isherwood

Biblical quotations are from the Catholic Edition of the Revised Standard Version of the Bible, © 1966 by the Division of Christian Education of the National Council of the Churches of Christ in the U.S.A.

Printed in the United States of America on acid-free paper

04 03 02 01 00 99   5 4 3 2 1

Library of Congress Cataloging-in-Publication Data

Isherwood, Lisa.
    Liberating Christ : exploring the christologies of contemporary liberation movements / Lisa Isherwood.
        p.   c.m.
    Includes bibliographical references and index.
    ISBN 0-8298-1350-0 (pbk : alk. paper)
    1. Liberation theology. 2. Jesus Christ—Person and offices.
I. Title.
BT83.57.I84 1999
232—dc21   99-30822
                                                                      CIP

CONTENTS

Foreword   vii

Acknowledgments   ix

1. Liberating Landscapes   1

2. Black, African, and Womanist Christologies   22

3. Jesus Christ Liberator?   48

4. Redeemer or Redeemed?   68

5. Queering Christ   89

6. Christ among the Shamans   110

7. Liberating Power, Liberating Praxis   128

Notes   151

Index   161

FOREWORD

Rosemary Radford Ruether

Lisa Isherwood has written an engaging and accessible introduction to the plethora of contemporary liberation Christologies. The central issue that underlies and motivates all these diverse Christologies is that Christology itself has historically been used as an instrument of oppression and hence needs to be liberated in order to regain its original meaning as a vision and vehicle of redemptive life.

Christology is the central symbol of the Christian faith. Faith that Jesus is the Christ, the *Messias*, the one who redeems humanity from bondage to sin and evil, is what makes Christianity distinctive. Thus it is the more scandalous that it is precisely through Christology that the Christian church has most often rationalized the perpetuation and enforcement of sin and evil!

The list of Christologies of oppression is long. There is the anti-Semitic Christ. This is the Christ of the *adversus Judaeos* tradition of the church fathers, rooted in the New Testament Christological interpretation of Hebrew Scripture. In the name of this Christ Christians have been called to repudiate the Jews as people who always rejected and killed the prophets and followed this same evil course in rejecting and killing Christ. For this sin God has rejected them and decreed that they were to be despised wanderers throughout the earth until they repent and accept Jesus as their Messiah. Christians are here mandated to be the instrument of God's punishing wrath against the Jews.

There is the imperial Christ of Eusebius of Caesaria and the theology of Christendom. This Christ is the *Pantocrator*, the All-Ruler of the universe who delegated the Christian Roman emperors to be his representatives. Christ here embodies the principles of imperial monarchy, mandating his representatives, Christian emperors and kings, to subdue and rule over all nations. In the name of this imperial Christ European Christendom sent the Crusaders in the eleventh and twelfth centuries to subdue the Muslims, and waves of colonizers in the sixteenth and seventeenth centuries to take over lands of the Americas, Asia, and Africa, making their people serf or slave laborers in order to carry their riches back to European banks. The result has been a mass pillaging of the globe that still continues today.

The imperialist Christ is also a racist, classist Christ in whose image black and brown people of the globe are denied full humanity and capacity to order their own affairs. He is the sexist Christ who can only be a male because only males can represent full humanity and "headship" over inferiors, specifically women. In the name of this white masculinist Christ women are declared to be unable to "image" Christ and hence cannot be Christ's "representative" in the ordained ministry.

The starting point for deconstructing this anti-Semitic, imperialist, racist, sexist Christ in liberation theologies has been a reencounter with the historical Jesus, who proclaimed his mission to be "good news to the poor, the liberation of the captives, the setting at liberty of those who are oppressed." Each new community of distress connects its story with the Jesus story in its own context. For Latin Americans it has been the message of "preferential option for the poor." Blacks have been empowered by a Christ who calls for setting the captives free. Women see Jesus as the one who sided with despised, low-status women of his time in critique of the proud caste of the righteous. Gays, too, look to Jesus as one who stands outside conventional family relations and can be sympathetic to their oppression.

As Lisa Isherwood makes clear, these many Christs are rooted in a historical Jesus with a liberating, prophetic bent, but they are more than literally historical. Indeed, a literally historical Jesus would have soon become useless, an interesting minor Jewish teacher of the first century who ran afoul of the local leaders and colonizing rulers. The power of Jesus to be liberating Christs for each new day and context lies in the coupling of a powerful memory of one who lived and died for justice with each new community's liberative action.

It is through this process that Jesus continues to rise from the dead, to be ever and again present with us as a "family story" that can spur us to imagine our fullest humanity freed from all forms of oppression. In this book Lisa Isherwood takes us on a fascinating global journey through the many sibling branches of this family that ever and again seek the fullness of redemptive freedom.

ACKNOWLEDGMENTS

I wish to thank Professor Adrian Thatcher of the University College of St. Mark and St. John, Plymouth, England, for his constant support and encouragement. I also wish to thank Professor Rosemary Radford Ruether for so kindly inviting me as the Georgia Harkness Visiting Scholar to Garrett-Evangelical Seminary, Evanston, Illinois, and for being such an inspiration and support during that time. Last, but by no means least, I wish to express my thanks to Timothy Staveteig of The Pilgrim Press for his kind words of encouragement.

1

LIBERATING LANDSCAPES

I recall a political cartoon some years ago that featured a panel of Jesus images. On the left was a haggard-looking man with a crown of thorns, nail marks on his hands, and blood seeping down his forehead. On the right was a beaming, muscular man with flowing hair and a confident chin. Two or three other figures were positioned somewhere in between on this continuum. The caption read, "Will the real Jesus please stand up?"

Today we can picture that each of these figures could stand up at once claiming to be the real Jesus. No one can describe with any certainty the details of Jesus' life or specify precisely his relation with God. This uncertainty in Christology crept in during the twentieth century after Albert Schweitzer showed how each of the great portraits of Jesus looked more like the scholar than like each other. Biblical scholars in the last hundred years have become increasingly circumspect about the real Jesus and his real words. Today Jesus Seminar scholars have found few authentic utterances of Jesus recorded in the Gospels.[1] Not that faith has leaked out of the Christian enterprise. Scholars for the past two thousand years have at one time or another, and on one issue or another, expressed concerns and even doubts. Yet they are also more willing to seek out a portrait of Christ that befits their situations and questions. Perhaps the difference between then and now is that more people today are willing to contemplate such concerns.

What has leaked out is a naive view of history. Once each event was viewed as a fact, an unchangeable thing. Today no historical moment can be viewed as fact, even as it unfolds. We have become comfortable with the idea of history as an assemblage of perceptions and interpretations—subject to reinterpretation or new packaging. Even where and when we might find fulcrums and levers for life have shifted. For example, many people are looking less to the first century in search of a radical rabbi who teaches with authority and more to the spirit of their own times in search of the radical and liberating alternatives available under their own particular oppression. On what basis can such a shift take place? Many understand an early title for Jesus—Emmanuel, "God with us"—as the promise of his continued redemptive action in the present.

Some will argue that we need to return to a naive view of history so that Christians can worship and promote the same Jesus. No panel of Jesus figures, just one. Yet this panel or diversity was evident even in the beginning of the Jesus movement. When Jesus asked the question, "Who do people say that I am?" (Mark 8:27), he got a range of answers. Instead of pressing Peter for a consensus, Jesus pressed him for his own understanding. Jesus was seeking an engagement with his way of being rather than a distillation of his one, true essence. Liberationists described in this book take this as Jesus' method of applying his way of being to the diversity of people's lives. The incarnation ("God becoming flesh") for them is far from divine genetic engineering; it is a way to find a liberating spirit and praxis for their times in the diversity of life.

A VARIETY OF CHRISTOLOGIES

What many modern-day Christians consider to be orthodox Christology is in fact an amalgam of the different interpretations and perceptions found in first-century Christianity. The preexistence theme in the Gospel of John is mixed with the virgin birth noted in the Gospel of Matthew and death as atonement from Paul's letters. Added to this conceptual stew is Hellenistic Christianity's divine man who enters human flesh and (later) who will return again.

This is a modest selection from the eighty or so "gospels" that were written by early Christians of various sorts. This fuller range illustrates the diversity of the different Christologies. That the so-called orthodox view is comprised of a limited selection gives us a clue for current theological work. The loss of historical facticity should not discourage us. As with the ancients, we have imagination and interpretation of a wide range of sources as ways of moving forward. Indeed, the current-day theologian's task is to seek a Christology for our time and place.[2]

More than a few theologians would rather understand Christianity's early years as a movement from plurality to orthodoxy under the firm guidance of the Spirit—a journey from darkness to absolute truth.

These theologians still cheer the rally of their bright, beaming, muscular Jesus to stand up as the only real Christ. But even a superficial understanding of the history of the Jesus movement shows the error in this view.

The missionaries after Jesus' death did not preach one message or expound one set of fixed doctrines. For example, not all those who advocated following Jesus thought it necessary to expound a view of divine conception and virgin birth. Many considered such views outrageous and absurd. The author of the Gospel of Philip, to name one, stated that a woman could not conceive by another woman (the Spirit being imaged as female). Others, such as Paul and the author of the Gospel of Mark, ignored any notion of a virgin birth. Followers of Jesus did not feel compelled to hold fixed and uniformly accepted ideas about his nature or about how exactly to make concrete his way of life.

Unity of doctrine became important when Christianity was made the Roman Empire's official religion in the early 300s C.E. by Constantine. The decision was political more than religious; the Romans found it much easier to govern peoples united by common belief, and Christianity seemed to be heartier than emperor worship. Some Christian leaders, however, took the opportunity to promote their doctrinal beliefs as constitutive of true belief. After having experienced several periods of persecution—the last and most horrific period beginning in 303 C.E., when the empire was threatened by Germanic bands, and ending in the Edict of Milan, 313 C.E.—Christians would specify who were in the group and who were the outcasts. Perhaps Christians felt responsible for the viability of the empire and thought that a pure worship could sustain its preeminence.[3]

Whatever the reasons, Christianity adopted the model of the empire by becoming more hierarchical and formal and by jettisoning much of its original charisma and prophecy. Divergent thinking was no longer tolerated. Jesus was handed over to the Romans once again, this time to become transformed into a power broker, a divine Caesar used to manipulate worldly power and to judge between life and death. The haggard-looking radical rabbi hanging from a cross became a symbol of imperial power.

With this turn, Christianity suddenly discovered heretics. The word "heresy" comes from the Greek *hairesis,* meaning "an act of free choice." Heretics introduced choices (or we might say, options) into Christian faith—defects, it was said, that were not from the beginning. Later usage represented heretics as either malicious subverters of the true faith or deluded fools, many of whom were in league with the devil.[4]

Many of the movements declared heretical—the Gnostics, for example—were led by women or had positive views about the role of women. Because women fulfilled a secondary function in Roman society, and therefore underpinned it, perhaps we should not be surprised that the growing religious hierarchies would treat as undesirable any movement that elevated the role of women.[5]

What was declared heretical seems even to the disinterested observer to be a movable feast. For example, Arius, an Alexandrian presbyter (died c. 335 C.E.), maintained that the Christ who was born, suffered, and died could not be one with the transcendent first cause of creation who is beyond all suffering. His views were condemned by the Council of Nicaea (325 C.E.), which set forth the trinitarian Nicene Creed. (Creeds are power tools that were considered unnecessary in the early movement.) At the Council of Rimini (359 C.E.), a group of Arian bishops came to power and defined Arian creeds that temporarily replaced the Nicene Creed. This council was overturned by the Council of Constantinople (381 C.E.).

JESUS AS A SOURCE FOR CHRISTOLOGY

Turning to Jesus the man is no help either, even when scholars agree on an item. At one time, for example, it was considered useful to underscore that Jesus was a Jew. Now we know that it tells us little about him because dozens of forms of Judaism were practiced in his day and because he does not appear to fit precisely into any of them. Or all considered true that Jesus' message was unique, but that no longer seems the case. Although not fitting any exact category within Judaism, Jesus seems to reflect many of the strands that were already in existence.[6]

The more we come to know about the world and belief systems of the first century, the less we are able to set Jesus in a place of superiority. Recent scholarship reflects these new insights with scholars such as Dominic Crossan and Burton Mack wishing to view the historical Jesus as a shrewd peasant teacher who challenged all the existing forms of the social order. Crossan claims that Jesus never wished to be the center of the message he was proclaiming but wanted people to engage with a liberating God in a more direct way. For Crossan, the Gospel of Thomas is the nearest we will get to an original since even Mark reworked the evidence in the light of particular Jewish understandings.[7]

Although Crossan and others feel that a case can be made on the grounds of the evidence provided, they are also aware that the first century is largely obscured from our view by giant filters: the filters of gender, wealth/power, and education. The traditions passed through the hands and the mental constructs of the upper echelons of society and have not come to us untainted by that passage.

Another problem for us is that our understanding of monotheism is rather different from the understanding in the first century. For a Jew to believe in one God was not to exclude the possibility of others but to assert the power of one's own. In the general worldview of the first century, gods and human beings were much closer; the dividing line between heaven and earth was more transparent and permeable than we imagine it to be today. We have become thoroughly dualistic in a way unimaginable to most people of that time. However, hints in the Christian writings show how flexible these worlds were. The writer of Hebrews encouraged his readers to treat strangers with hospitality because they might be angels (Heb. 13:2), while we learn from Acts that Paul was declared a god because he was bitten by a viper and did not die (Acts 28:6) and Barnabas and Paul were at different times thought to be Zeus and Hermes (Acts 14:10–13). This reminds us that such titles as God and Child of God were spoken in a different context and carried different meanings.[8]

We are unable to ask only one Jesus on the panel to rise up as the real one. We have historical material, but it is slimmer and less clear than we first thought. To look at this positively, we can say that we have enough to proceed but not enough to get bogged down in certainty. The man Jesus of Nazareth was tortured and killed because he challenged the existing order, and most accounts show that he cared for persons in need and did his best to alleviate their suffering in the here and now. The early writers grappled with the meaning of this within their context, and the fragments that we have allow us to understand that there was no one orthodox view—there was midrash, a constant flow of contrast and correctives. The aim of this engagement was the expansion of redemptive praxis.

WHAT CHRISTOLOGY IS

Christology is finding redemptive praxis in one's own history with no fear of diversity and change. Using this understanding, we are able to see how the various Christologies of liberation are modern-day versions of the struggles and tensions that existed in the early Jesus movement when charisma and transformation were the major issues and orthodoxy was of less importance. This book attempts to illustrate how various liberation theologies have approached Christology and how they have added to the interpretation in the hope of reclaiming Christ from death by doctrinal fossilization.

LATIN AMERICA AS THE BASE MODEL

At the Medellín Conference in Colombia in 1968, the Roman Catholic Latin American bishops openly challenged the situations of injustice and poverty in their countries. As Gustavo Gutiérrez subsequently reflected, theology attempts to answer questions about God, but these are now coming from our everyday situations: "We are dealing with the classic question of the relation between faith and human existence, between faith and social reality, between faith and political action, or in other words between the kingdom of God and the building of the world."[9]

Gutiérrez and other theologians rightly refused to rely on metaphysical speculation to answer the hard questions. They also resisted the strong call to view the world as evil, but chose instead to change it in the direction of the realm of God. Their task was to address their context in which colonizing powers were still creating a situation of economic dependency despite the crushing effects on the vast majority of the people. An imperial version of Christianity robbed the people of identity, land, and liberty and placed them in a position of dependency, a position often underpinned by religion.

Liberation theologians began with the incarnation because it shows that history matters. They argued that the Hebrew Scriptures clearly show a God who works in and through the historical processes—salvation is an event, or possibly many events, in history. The life of Jesus, which was embedded in the Hebrew understanding of God, was one in which he illustrated how to become children of God. Thus, even our personal history is of significance in the salvific process. Each personal life is graced and free, and the world is in a state of becoming rather than of disintegration. Such optimism about human nature is biblically based, remembering that God created all things and saw they were good (Gen. 1:31). Further, the freedom with which we have been endowed can work to make things better.

Further reflection on the exodus of the people of Israel shows that salvation is a joint historical event: God acted with the people to change their situation. God did not do it all for them but walked with them on their path to freedom. Human forces were instrumental in the change from captivity to freedom. This same move to freedom for the oppressed can be witnessed in the life of Jesus. He engaged people in the process of their own liberation through stories, healings, and conversations. Thus, Christians do not simply have to pray for the world but have to change it, and this assumes that we are capable of good.

If we accept that this commitment to justice and freedom is evident in the pages of the Bible, then we will be filled with moral outrage when we see that it is not happening in large areas of life. And we will be moved to act. Liberation theologians are wise enough to know that one person cannot take on all the injustice in the world, and so part of the methodology of liberation theology is to acknowledge both universality and preference. The former acknowledges the universal love of God, declaring that those who oppress are not outside God's love—and any struggle for freedom is as interested in freeing those who oppress as those who are oppressed. The latter encourages people to take a stance, to declare their preference, in one area of the struggles for justice. By this focusing of energy, more is achieved than through getting overwhelmed with the complex multiplicity of needs evident in our world.

Struggles for justice should not be compartmentalized, however. A great deal of strength is to be gained through understanding the common threads running through various forms of oppressive behavior and regimes. Latin American theology makes a preferential option for the poor, seeing this as God's option. The poor are the central focus of this theology not because they are in any way better than others but because the biblical message is one of justice. Within the Latin American context the poor are persons suffering the most crushing injustice. In other contexts poverty may be the consequence of other oppressions, such as gender, which will need to be equally addressed.

Because of its emphasis on poor people and their place in underpinning elitist systems, Latin American theology has often been accused of being Marxist rather than Christian. It is certainly materialist in both its approach to understanding social dynamics and the way in which it analyzes sin as social/systemic reality. Marx wrote more about economic reality than Jesus did, so it may be useful to employ Marx in a search for economic justice.

It is always helpful if social theory is able to highlight how misfortunes and oppressions, which we have been led to believe are private, are shown to be products of the way society is set up. Once the problem is situated in society and not personal moral weakness, we are a step nearer finding a liberative way forward. Marx was interested in describing how things functioned and why they functioned that way. His conclusion that capitalist economics places antagonism at the heart of social relations, a method ensuring that only the needs of the elite are truly served, is as valid today as in his own time. With the frightening growth of multinational companies his analysis is truer today than ever.

A return to precapitalist modes of production, which some liberation theologians are advocating in an attempt to escape further Western exploitation, is no answer to the problems faced, even if it were possible to turn back the clock in such a way. It is also not a Marxist solution. Marx actually found capitalism to be the first step to socialism because he understood that the generation of wealth is necessary. Where he parted company with the dominant philosophy was that he did not see it as an end in itself; to him, it was a tool that could be used to alleviate exploitation. The issue, then, is how to generate income in such a way as to benefit all. Latin America and many other countries are on the receiving end of brutal capitalist exploitation, and Marx does not have all the answers for that situation, as we will see, but his analysis is helpful for understanding the web of oppression.

The notion of developed and underdeveloped countries was still one frame of reference within the Medellín Conference. But there also emerged the Marxist idea of dependency and domination. The so-called dependency theory is a tool for describing the way in which certain countries are made dependent on others through economic and political means. This makes them vulnerable to manipulation both internally and externally. How this is achieved varies according to context; therefore, the dependency theory outlines a principle more than a fixed set of options. Helder Camara, among others, for example, was able to speak of internal and external colonialism and to express both as collective sin.[10] This emergent understanding was able to shift the emphasis of the debate from that of addressing issues of underdevelopment to that of imaging liberation. The bishops at the conference did not have a sudden conversion to uncritical Marxism. Indeed, they were concerned by how many working people were attracted to communism. Yet they recognized that capitalism, not individual moral weakness, was crushing the same people. They were willing to be informed by sociologists as much as by Scripture in an effort to find liberating alternatives.

A range of analyses emerged that showed how economics, ideology, and politics are shaped by external pressures working in their own exploitative interests. Despite the lack of cohesion between these theories, that was the first attempt to see Latin American reality through Latin American eyes and not through the lens of Western capitalist theory. Such capitalism has an inherent dualism between traditional and modern society in which underdevelopment means backwardness in culture and lack of sophistication in technology. Yet orthodox Marxism has an inherent dualism between the traditional feudal and bourgeois industrial society.[11]

Despite its drawbacks, the dependency theory has been a useful tool to help in understanding the way in which both internal and external forces are operating to keep poor people marginalized and with little hope. It enables people to think in terms of action, not passive acceptance. If a system is constructed, then it can be deconstructed. Dependency theory by liberation theologians fuels the push for liberation through militant action. Marxist theory helps liberation theology to understand class conflict, to formulate liberative action, and to be suspicious of dominant ideas because they will probably serve only the elite. This is also true with dominant theologies, not just political rhetoric.

Labeling persons as Marxists is a convenient weapon in the armory of the opponents of liberation theology. Camara underscores this absurdity: Why is it, he wonders, that he is called a saint if he speaks *about* the poor, but a Communist if he asks *why* they are poor?[12] The reasons for poverty need economic as well as theological investigation.

To hasten the ending of exploitation, liberation theologians replaced Aristotle with Marx because they found Marx's adage to be true: philosophers merely describe the world while Marxist theory aims to change it.[13] But inherent in the Aristotelian description is a dualistic understanding that subordinates the reality of this world to that of a higher spiritual realm. This makes urgent radical material change of little consequence. Camara and others, despite giving an ear to Marxism, still viewed the radical gospel as central in the motivation for the change, and they considered it able to bring about the desired revolution. The goal of such a revolution is not a Marxist utopia, but the gospel reality.

All of this had repercussions for Catholic theologians who also sought to work within ecclesial structures. The church was able to dodge questions about the way in which it conducts its economic affairs. But it has felt keenly efforts to destabilize the church as a static hierarchy of continuities and to conceive itself more as a church that grows out of the people. Under such a grassroots model, the church would be constantly changing and growing as the needs of people change. The Curia of the Roman Catholic Church has responded to this transforming suggestion by saying that it is hierarchical by divine institution and that hierarchical ministry is essentially bound up with the sacrament of order.[14]

In a prior time, such institutional caution might have stifled the movement. In Latin America, such decrees meant that people went ahead anyway without further consultation with the hierarchy. The search for new ways of being church led to the development of base communities that are small, face-to-face groups in which people celebrate communion and reflect on Scripture together within their own context. Dissatisfaction on the margins of urban areas met with a vulnerability and an opportunity—a shortage of priests and a push, after Vatican II, to include the laity in more areas of church life. Certainly, many of the bishops who supported the movement did so in the hope of evangelizing more people through the work of nuns and lay catechists. But as has been the case in all liberation groups, new ecclesiologies have almost instinctively emerged.

Many of the Latin American groups came together in the face of extreme opposition. Governments resorted to violence with catechists often being killed, while in certain areas whole groups were massacred for owning a Bible. Much of the church hierarchy remained silent. More than a few sought to discredit liberation theology by calling it secular and claiming that its practitioners supported violence. The blood being shed was that of the poor and weak; these martyrs are seen as witnessing to another way of being church, and their memory is fuel for the continued struggle.

Despite such opposition, the marginalized of society gathered to be the basic moving force in the struggles for their own liberation. Small groups made it possible for people to really be part of the community through sharing responsibility for social as well as political action.[15] In this way reflection on Scripture and tradition, on the one hand, and the concrete experiences of people, on the other, made it possible to formulate action and resistance. The base communities began to realize that the Bible was really their book because it told stories that reflected many of the realities of their lives.

Clodovis Boff has examined this so-called hermeneutic mediation. The people always begin from a real question that is based in their everyday reality. They are then helped to understand the problem through the intervention of social science or, failing that, a theologian. This social situation is brought in relation to Scripture with the whole community working together to find meaning first for the text and then in their lived experience. This practical-pastoral-political mediation is circular in nature because each step of the cycle leads to the next.[16]

When the texts are placed back in the hands of poor people, the central focus shifts away from clerics and theologians and their methods shaped by dominant power structures. This is not to suggest that the base communities are cut off from the institutional church, but that the focus is on what the institution can do for the poor instead of what they do for the institution. This shift does not romanticize the poor but acknowledges that possibly the central aim of the life of Jesus was to bring good news to the poor—and what better news than they are poor no more, captives of domination no more, and so on. The way in which the base communities celebrate sacraments and reflect on Scripture together has inspired many other groups around the globe, for example, women church and gay and lesbian church groups.

THE BASE EXPANDS

Latin American liberation theology caught the imagination of others around the world who perceived their own situations to be oppressive. However, far from being accepted with open arms by these groups, the Latin American movement was challenged by those who claimed that the vision was not broad enough. The rumblings began as early as 1975 when it started to become plain that liberation was not the same thing for all people.

The Marxist analysis that was influential in the theology of Latin America could not be uncritically applied to other situations, for example, where race and gender were the main issues. There was strong criticism that liberation theologians, in focusing so intently on the poor, had failed to think of the situation of women and blacks. Questions were raised regarding the implications for these groups, and in the process the prophetic vision of the initial model and the limitations of the vision were exposed. Most groups could agree that economic injustice was an issue for them, but many also concluded that economic injustice was not the whole of their story. A realization began to dawn that colonization was cultural as well as economic and that to make the gospel of liberation meaningful it had to be expressed in cultural, linguistic, and symbolic ways that were free of European androcentric thought forms.[17]

EATWOT (Ecumenical Association of Third World Theologians) was founded to provide a platform on which to discuss liberation theology. Within this forum many of the difficulties began to surface and be faced. Before the EATWOT conference in São Paulo in 1980, women, groups of indigenous peoples, and blacks discussed fully the ways in which oppression affected them in order to bring the issues to the attention of the conference. Among other things, women pointed to the macho ideology prevalent in Latin America that contributed to their lack of self-esteem. Indigenous peoples drew attention to their struggles for land rights and the difficulties of preserving their cultures. Black people raised the question of culture and identity and the crushing effects of whiteness, that is, seeing things through white eyes and considering this to be the superior or ideal way of doing things.

It would be encouraging to say that Latin American liberation theologians embraced these deliberations with enthusiastic openness, but that was not the case. For many it was not until preparations for the five-hundred-year anniversary of the colonization of the Americas in 1992 that the realization dawned of the plight of their own indigenous peoples.[18] To place these comments in perspective, lack of concern was not motivated by imperialistic thinking as much as by a fear that the other side issues would divert liberation theology from challenging the real evil of economic injustice.

In many ways these fears have been realized because there has been an explosion of concerns and cultural contexts under the umbrella of liberation theology. The questions raised are no longer simply economic, but they all focus on the need for liberation. African theology, for example, seeks to take seriously an African worldview, which does not just add the trappings of African culture to an otherwise Eurocentric Christianity. It attempts to value the land and root its theology in African ideas of community. It aims to overcome the African Christian schizophrenia that was brought about because the African soul was not being reached by a white cerebral religion, which gave answers to questions that would never be asked from the African context.[19]

There are dangers in overemphasizing the African soul in the sense that it can play into the hands of the nationalist ruling classes. This is not desirable because the goal is to liberate people from all oppression, not merely to change the context of the oppression. Oppression is no better because it is perpetrated by one's own people. African theology aims to create theology that not only comes out of the culture but also is accountable to the culture. Its critique of imperialist religion feeds into current political situations where imperialism is still prevalent in development programs and global economics. South African theologians are only too well aware that although one liberation battle, that against apartheid, is won, there are many more to be fought.

The global healing desired by African theologians requires both an ecological and an economic metanoia through which old problems are addressed and new, visionary answers found that have equality at their heart. The old models that led to imperialist thinking will no longer suffice. Before demanding that equity become a global principle, the men of Africa have to embrace the equality of women, which is not an easy task for some. African women carry the extra burden of gender in societies that have often been more concerned with the global picture than with the injustices in the home. The women of Africa are developing a Christology of human empowerment that is already shaking the foundations of male privilege.

Asian theology has a totally different setting, that of a living pluralism in the society. The challenge is to create a space in which Christianity can speak with the great Asian religious traditions such as Taoism and Buddhism. It has to learn to speak humbly and no longer with an imperialistic voice. The diverse cultures of Asia pose a range of challenges to Christianity, and it must not fear losing its Western identity if real progress is to be made. Asian theology has a common theme of siding with the poor and the suffering, which Christianity has to deal with contextually. But importing concepts to place plaster over the cracks will not do. Christianity must not live under the illusion that it will be unchanged when it hears the diverse voices from Asia.

Perhaps the strongest voices are those belonging to women. As in other contexts, they have borne the brunt of an unjust system with their oppression springing from their own cultures as well as those of the colonizers. The women of India, Korea, Hong Kong, and the Philippines are critiquing two oppressive cultures because their lives literally depend on it. They are involved in a complex dance of survival, picking their way with creative imagination through the close-knit web of colonial and precolonial oppression that shapes their everyday lives. Like some of their African sisters, they understand that ecology is inextricably linked with Christology. They cannot be liberated if the land on which they live is exploited; the bond between women and nature demands a Christ who can save the cosmos.

The women of Latin America, Africa, and Asia also began confronting their male colleagues about their lack of gender awareness in relation to economic realities. Vandana Shiva highlights how women, who are producing for survival and not profit, are sidelined when development programs are introduced and their knowledge is disregarded. They become more dispossessed, and the knowledge that they had passed to them about the needs of their own environment is lost forever, often with devastating consequences. When control and profit take the upper hand, "women and nature working to produce and reproduce life are declared 'unproductive'"[20] and are linked in a downward spiral. They also raised questions about gender-specific forms of oppression, such as lack of contraceptive choice, sexual violence, and restrictions in education, employment, and church functions.

Male liberation theologians initially ignored the liberative needs of women and were not immediately convinced that they should be addressed. In 1982, due to the, at best, lukewarm responses of their male colleagues, the EATWOT women set up their own Women's Commission to address feminist theology within distinct contexts.[21] The commission facilitated consultations between women of Latin America, Africa, and Asia, and in 1994 they entered into dialogue with the women of the First World—the conversation is still going strong. The aim is to understand both similarities and differences in oppression and, if possible, to find common strategies for resistance.

Through focus on Third World women's oppression, a whole new area opened up, that of ecological concerns. Colonization involved the enslavement of land as well as people, and women who depend on land for survival are best placed to point out the liberative needs of the earth itself. Vandana Shiva and others graphically illustrate that even so-called Third World development programs are inventions of the purveyors of advanced capitalism. They have created great affluence for the few, usually male, and have done so at great cost to the already dispossessed, who are largely women. These programs have no respect for traditional ways of working and do not understand the crucial difference between productivity for survival and productivity for profit.[22] The challenge is to maintain the connection of women and nature but to reverse the fortunes of both. The poisoning and impoverishment of Third World people through exploitative use of their land by the so-called developed world raises many questions of liberation for both land and people.

Western women are in solidarity with their sisters in other parts of the world and share the same concerns, yet many of the specific questions they need to face are quite different. Perhaps the most pressing is how to act for life in systems that are so advanced in capitalism that such choices are not easily accomplished. Western women have won many employment opportunities over the last fifty years, but they do not have a great deal of power to actually change the way in which, for example, large corporations work. Western feminists are in a double-bind situation; to succeed, they have to play the game, but when they do succeed, their power to effect change is limited and so they are part of the crushing reality of Western capitalism.

The major question that faces Western women in the new millennium is how to take power in a new and freeing way, a way that empowers all. Eastern European women are facing the stark reality of capitalism since the fall of the Soviet bloc, and many have only their bodies left to sell—such is the debilitating effect of this so-called democratizing form of economics. The promises of Hollywood-type lifestyles have manifested grinding poverty coupled with little hope. Perhaps the greatest challenge will emerge from this new victim of capitalism since there is nothing to lose and there are recent memories of other ways.

Until recently, all theologies of liberation have ignored issues of homophobia, which appears to be the last acceptable prejudice. Emerging gay and lesbian theologies challenge the received wisdom about their state and call to account churches that have failed to stand by them in the various struggles of their lives. In addition to confronting institutionalized homophobia, gay and lesbian theology poses questions about the nature of sexuality and patterns of human relating. There is a growing awareness that gay and lesbian theologies do not have the same concerns. Although certain common strategies may be employed, there are many differences that are based on gender. Much work needs to be done to sensitize men to the issues of women and to help gay and lesbian people to overcome their own internalized homophobia.

The guidance given by most churches is of little real help to gays and lesbians who encounter the devastating and debilitating myopia of many parts of society. Gay and lesbian responses to institutional oppression take two broad forms. The first is to attempt to be normative through conforming to traditional Christian patterns of life. That is calling for gay marriage and so on. The second approach is more confrontational—presenting gay and lesbian lifestyles as challenges to traditional patterns. This queer challenge demands an expansion of Christological understanding to encompass the lived realities of gay life.

Many of the struggles for liberation, which have an economic understanding at their base, have received a severe blow since the collapse of the Berlin Wall. This is not because a role model has failed. Liberation theologians were always aware of the weaknesses in the Soviet system. There are more practical implications. An alternate source of funding for resistance movements and small Communist governments has dried up, and the victors, Western capitalism, can now create all the economic rules by which everybody must play. There is a real sense in which economic alternatives have been eliminated and the world is at the mercy of advanced capitalism. There is no longer any need to pretend that Western capitalism eventually intended to include Third World countries in the bounty sharing.[23]

As I write, the United States is riding high on an economic wave while markets crash around it with dire consequences for those who are already disadvantaged in the developing world. The policies of the United States are blatantly exploitative, for example, of Latin America, and they will go to any lengths to ensure continued dependency, even through funding civil war. Despite being found guilty of illegal involvement in the contra wars in Nicaragua and being ordered by the World Court to pay $17 billion in damages, the United States refuses to pay and continues to increase the economic pressures.[24] Nicaragua became the poorest country in Central America, although it now has all the trappings of affluence, such as shopping malls and health centers. The people cannot afford to shop or to pay for health care, however. This pattern is spreading throughout Latin America, aided by free trade agreements and negative interventions of the World Bank.[25]

Latin American liberation theologians are witnessing genocide that is a consequence of unleashing the many-headed beast of advanced capitalism. Workers who are no longer necessary to create obscene profits are starving to death or succumbing to disease due to poor nutrition.

Many of the economic resources necessary for a Marxist form of resistance are gone, and new ways have to be found to resist. On the day the North American Free Trade Agreement (NAFTA) was signed, the poor people of Mexico made their presence felt in the uprising at Chiapas. Their action was at least a sign that people will not lie down under the new world order but will demand to be seen and heard.[26]

This desire to find alternate visions, even in extreme circumstances, is the incarnational spirit that governments and at times Christianity have tried to contain or destroy. Is it too outrageous to suggest that the church, rather than indulging in the advantages of dominant economics, should be fully involved in developing and sustaining another economic reality? One that learns from the past, gives life in the present, and offers hope for the future for the majority, not just the few. Despite its apparent thriving, capitalism cannot sustain itself indefinitely; therefore, alternatives have to be sought in order to liberate the present and sustain the future. Economic involvement is not an option for Christians; it is an imperative, even for those who do not consider themselves liberation theologians.

A SHARED METHODOLOGY

Despite their unique contexts, liberation theologies have a shared methodology that allows them to hang together. Although there has been some implicit handling of methodology in this chapter, it would not be amiss to make some explicit points about what constitutes liberation methodology. This focus will help the contours of the liberation landscape to emerge.

The first and most obvious point is that liberation theologies are committed to doing theology contextually. This should not be confused with a privatized form of doing theology because the context mentioned here can never stop at the boundary of one's own skin. Context refers to social location and is a category that can be shared by others in one's group who will suffer the same restrictions because of it.

For example, femaleness, blackness, or gayness are not just individual characteristics. They also set an agenda for how groups of people will be treated in the world and the avenues that will be open to them. The agenda and the avenues are social and economic realities as much as they are physical attributes, and they provide the context for liberation theology.

Liberation theology challenges the dominant ideologies of the in group that underpin the exclusions or oppressions affecting various out groups. Since all knowledge is constructed, it can be deconstructed through the employment of social science, economics, and radical theology. Some forms of liberation theology prefer to keep away from this kind of intellectual engagement and work instead at the level of narrative. Much Asian (Minjung) theology thrives on extending the imaginative bounds of theological and social culture rather than through intellectual critical engagement. All liberation theologies, however, have transformation as the goal—the transformation of unjust systems into just and inclusive ones.

Liberation theologies do not operate in tight and rigid categories. It is quite possible to be a poor black lesbian. Such a woman would not benefit from a purely Marxist analysis of her situation or a feminist one that had no concept of race. This woman's situation requires multiple levels of analysis and a many-layered pattern of resistance. Until recently, there has not always been this comprehension of the many layers and complexions of oppression; there was a rather naive understanding that all oppression looked alike. However, most liberation theologians now realize that, for example, to be black carries one set of oppressions while to be a black lesbian carries another oppressive reality altogether. Further, there may be no economic oppression. Many lesbians are affluent, but their affluence does not necessitate free access to church and society.

Audre Lorde, the black lesbian activist and writer, observed how a black woman driving a Mercedes and living in Scarsdale is still seen as a black bitch in a racist, patriarchal society.[27] Her own situation amply highlighted the multiple layers of oppression in our complex societies. She was an affluent black woman who often found exclusion in white society for her color and in black society because of her sexuality. White lesbian society often reacted toward her out of sexual stereotypes rooted in a slave-owning past. Amidst all this she found happiness as a mother in a long-term mixed race partnership.

Liberation theology does not stop at describing and comprehending these layers of reality; it also requires action. To be more accurate, it engages in a process of reflection, action, reflection, and more action. This theology does not allow its practitioners to wallow in safe, contemplative bliss. They have to face harsh reality and attempt to change it. The movements for change have two consequences. Change occurs, and people come to see that they can bring about change. In this way ordinary people become transformed and empowered and understand that they are not merely passive victims in oppressive societies. The notion that salvation has a history, the one that we are living now, means that Christians have a responsibility to shape that history according to the liberative ideals of Jesus.

There has been a significant move in liberation theology toward admitting that Christian theology is not above perpetuating injustice. It contains many oppressive components; therefore, it cannot simply be the uncritical use of Christian theology that will liberate oppressed persons from worldly powers. Christianity has not only contributed to oppression by backing colonial powers, for example, by the church giving Catholic Spain the task of colonizing and converting the western half of the world and Catholic Portugal the task of doing the same for the eastern half of the world. Through many of its theological constructions, Christianity has also helped to create the mind-set in which abuse and oppression have been able to develop.

For example, the interpretation placed on the actions of Eve in Eden has led to centuries of venomous declarations about the nature of women and has underpinned the imposition of restrictions placed upon us. Women have been encouraged to mutilate themselves for Christ and to wear themselves out in the service of others. The Roman Catholic Church still operates Aristotelian forms of biology and metaphysics in order to consider the rightful place of women and to restrict their access to religious/secular space.

Liberation theologies are now as intent on dealing with this kind of internal oppression as they are with dealing with socioeconomic oppression. The foundations of Christianity may sometimes have to be shaken in order to discern what comes from the liberative praxis of Jesus and what originates in the inculturation of the gospel in the Greco-Roman world. Each area of theology is examined from Christology to eschatology, and each comes under the scrutiny of lived experience, not norms or theological givens. The Scriptures and traditions from which these theories arise are understood as belonging to the whole people of God and as such have to be interpreted in, by, and through justice-seeking communities. This turns traditional exegesis on its head since it was a form of practice carried out by the elite on behalf of the universal church. However, this can no longer be seen as a valid way to live out liberative/salvific history.

Praxis is a central concept in liberation theologies, which have been said to be more interested in orthopraxis than orthodoxy—and this is to a large extent true. By this it is meant that how one acts, the combination of faith and action, distinguishes a worthy system of belief from a corrupt one. Praxis is developed through the methodological approach outlined earlier, that is, through reflection, action, reflection, and action. This creates a fluid series of actions that respond to constantly changing situations rather than a rigid set of doctrines that are impervious to change. It acknowledges that human action makes a difference to human affairs. Situations never remain the same and so require constantly shifting perspectives and a variety of incarnate responses. Christians are therefore called to be flexible and creative in their engagement with the world. Underlying the whole notion of praxis is the clear belief that Jesus Christ, who engages with the world, is a liberator. The unchanging Thomist God has no place here.

LIBERATION AND CHRISTOLOGY

The various theologies of liberation are firmly underpinned by Christologies. Although they vary a great deal, they also have certain things in common. It will be useful to look at these commonalties before examining various Christologies in greater detail in other chapters.

First, a basic underlying assumption is that God is not neutral, but wants liberation for all people. This liberating God appears to give special attention to poor and marginalized people and demands justice for them. As Jean Marc Éla says, "When we take the side of the poor, we enter into a conspiracy with God, that is, we conspire against injustice."[28] The biblical God makes this a requirement. This God is a lover of justice, even if with hindsight God may regret some of the ways it was previously sought.

Second, this divine imperative for seeking justice among us is seen in the life of Jesus, who proclaimed the reign of God at hand. There was a great deal of eschatological expectation in his day (a coming judgment or visitation by God), so Jesus' own concern with it would be understandable. His slant on it was to make clear that the reign of God is established when God's will for justice, starting with advocacy for the poor, is sought. Solidarity with the poor was a sign of one's readiness for the coming of that reign. Jesus lived that way by including the excluded, healing the sick, and transforming people's understandings and their lives through his actions.

Third, the death of Jesus has always played a central role in Christian understanding. However, it has taken on a largely metaphysical meaning that loses its political implications. Jesus was a threat to the status quo because his actions proclaimed a more inclusive way of living. As with most threats to the state, he was exterminated in a way to inhibit further discontent. The bloody and protracted torture of a human being in a public place has only one objective, and that is to terrorize the general public into silence and obedience. To place this in the arena of metaphysics—to make it positive or useful as a part of salvation—is in many ways blasphemous. If the price for sin has already been paid, then it takes the pressure off us to act; we need only believe.

Fourth, liberation theologies are clear that salvation is not a passive thing; it is worked for and fought for every day that we live under unjust and oppressive systems. It involves people accepting their responsibility in the system and attempting to change it, so this requires both personal and political engagement with oppression.

Thus, the landscapes of liberation are multicolored and variously contoured. They encompass all areas of life and strive for the joyous bursting forth of life free and fulfilled. This is not a utopian dream since those who declare such an ecstatic revolution are aware of the pain and suffering that in many cases have to come before even the slightest move in the liberative direction. Nevertheless, this commitment is thought to be worthwhile because God created the world and saw it was good. This divine affirmation of creation underpins all movements for justice. It provides the assurance that all that is bad has been made so by human hands and therefore can be unmade by other human hands. Alternate realities are possible because there is a core goodness in the human heart. Battered and bruised as it may be, the heart can be resurrected through outrageous acts of kindness and undaunted justice seeking.

The liberation landscape is not that of the heavenly realm since such virtual reality is of little or no use in a bleeding world. What we see is the horizon of our struggle, but we are called to global vision. Human experience has always been the starting point for theological reflection, but the experience of the elite has become normative.

Liberation theology does not wish to objectify individual, or even group, experience in such a way. It has no wish to create symbols that dominate the universal landscape; it wishes to enable the springing up of fertile oases in many desolate wastelands. When each group settles under its own fig trees and harvests its own vines, the universal landscape will be radically transformed.

This is not by any means a call for separatist groups—merely an illustration that when people are allowed their space on the planet, a landscape of justice prevails, one in which the glorious diversity of creation shines brilliantly in all areas of life. Further, a common language is developed that overcomes the babbling silence of Babel; by this I mean that agendas are so diverse at present that despite the noise, there is deafening silence around the needs of people and the planet itself.

The common language that emerges is that of listening, the hearing one another to speech to which Nelle Morton alerted us.[29] We are to hear and act in a globally empowering way. It is a common effort from and for our common humanity, which promotes creative nonconformity. It is important always to resist settling into routines since they can become norms that are eventually used to impede individual growth. Creative nonconformity is not a convenient way of living—all modern conveniences and a high-tech exit to heaven when you die. It is instead a creative engagement with the planet and those who inhabit it, both human and nonhuman. It is a call to see each situation with new eyes and to act on it with empowered imagination. The subject of this book concerns how some of these imaginings have come into being.

2

BLACK, AFRICAN, AND WOMANIST CHRISTOLOGIES

B lack theology is the oldest political theology, even though it is not always recognized in this way. As long ago as 1700, a Congolese girl called Kimpa Vita prophetically proclaimed that Christ was black and had black apostles. This idea much later became central in the development of black theology and was one strand in the black communities' creation of theology to counter racism. This chapter focuses on the various strands in the web of that struggle, examining Christologies from Africa, Britain, and the African American context.

BLACK AFRICAN CHRISTOLOGIES

The African American leader W. E. B. DuBois, as early as 1903, could see that one of the biggest problems of the century would be racism.[1] A century later it is still difficult to make people appreciate just what that means. People tend to think of racism only in terms of individual acts of abuse or exclusion. Racism, however, is much more than that; it is systemic violence and exclusion. Further, it is perpetuated through a complex interplay of economic and political structures set in place by the elites in the defense of their own privilege. Exclusion on the grounds of physical characteristics has served the agenda of hierarchical power well. It goes without saying, then, that racism is a humanly constructed system and not rooted in any innate or divine absolute.

Racism and the Slave Experience Behind Black Theology

Slavery plays a significant part in the history of racism. The picture is not as clear as one may have assumed. Racism appears to be the result of slavery rather than the cause of it. The origin of slavery lies in economics, and even Aristotle is clear that those who are conquered in war may be used as slaves to aid production and profit in the nation-states. However, there was no racial element in his writing because those who were conquered in Greek wars were of many racial types. Eric Williams demonstrates that the first slaves in the New World were not picked due to racist ideology. The first slaves were Indians, followed closely by white men.[2] Neither race was productive enough; neither was strong enough to survive transportation or the physical exertion demanded in slave labor. Black slaves, on the other hand, particularly from the sub-Saharan region, were cheaper to acquire, there was a ready supply of them to be sold into slavery, and they were stronger, which meant that they survived transportation and the rigors of slavery. In short they were more cost-effective—such is the mentality behind slavery.

Racism, then, is one way in which people justify the use of others in slavery for economic advantage. Racism requires ideologies to be developed in all areas of life in order to hide the truth behind slavery. Unfortunately, religion was not immune to these fabrications. Justification for the enslavement of blacks can be found in the papal bulls of Nicholas V (1454) and Callistus III (1456). The reasoning behind these Christian documents was that enslaved pagans could be Christianized. The enslavement of their bodies was nothing compared to the freedom given their souls.

The theological revolution that was the Reformation did nothing to challenge the Catholic Church's view on slavery and, therefore, nothing for the position of slaves. Protestants developed their own reasoning regarding this matter and made the situation worse because theirs was a more Bible-based religion and they looked for and found biblical justification for racial oppression. At least the Catholic Church could decide that its reasoning had been wrong and do a complete turnaround at any moment. Some Calvinist Protestant theologians, in contrast, declared that black people were inferior by divine command.

One of the stories employed to draw this conclusion was that Ham, the son of Noah, was cursed by his father and doomed to slavery because Ham saw Noah's nakedness while Noah was drunk (Gen. 9:20–26). (The text seems confused about whether Canaan or Ham committed the offense, and which of them is cursed.) Africans were thought to be the descendants of Ham (taken literally as "dark"); by divine command they should be enslaved.

If darker peoples are to be enslaved, then one might ask about the skin color of Adam and Eve. The dominant white Protestant group saw the primal couple as God's intended ideal white pair. It was apparent to them that white is the ideal of creation because of their higher culture and godly worship. Blacks, because of the curse, embody vices. This construction of blackness as evil allowed whites to take whatever they disliked in themselves and project it onto the black races—savagery, lust, bestiality, sloth, and so on. Not without accident, the most oppressive forms of racism have been found in the most strictly Bible-believing and morally rigid groups, for example, Puritan Calvinists, Southern Baptists, and Dutch Reformed as found in South Africa and America.

The concepts of created and moral superiority made it possible for slaveholders to believe that they were participating in a divine calling to keep the bestial heathen in their place. Alternatively, they often felt that they were overseeing immature people who needed firm and often brutal guidance to keep them on the straight and narrow. The white Christian man was doing the black man a favor. There was little in Christian history to make him think otherwise. The church fathers had left the subject of slavery to one side because it formed the foundation of the Roman Empire. When Christianity was a marginal religion, it thought it could do little to change political ideology; when Christianity became enfranchised, it did not want to risk its political advantage over this issue.

When talking of brotherly and sisterly love and equality in Christ (Gal. 3:28), the early church understood this equality as a purely spiritual matter. Social position was the will of God and should remain unchallenged. This position only worsened under some forms of Protestant theology. Slavery was not seriously challenged as anti-Christian until the seventeenth century when some Quakers raised their voices against it. Methodists tried to take a stance by threatening to excommunicate those who did not free their slaves, but the power of slaveholders was so great that it proved nothing more than an idle threat in the end.

The slave rebellion of 1800—as well as those of subsequent years that were inspired by religion—solidified the dominant white position and made the case for reform harder. Slaveholders opposed even more vigorously baptizing slaves and preaching the gospel to them. Why? Doing so had led to social unrest. Those who still desired that slaves might become Christian argued that Christianity would make them more obedient. The gospel could work better than the whip. Mission work with slaves, then, became a means of social control.[3] Special catechisms were developed for slaves, which carried a specific agenda. For example, one catechism offered this typical encouragement: "Question: What did God make you for? Answer: To make a crop."[4]

Beginnings of Black Theology

White propaganda for obedience was challenged. Yet the important innovation was that slaves formulated their own approaches. Even though slaves were not allowed to read the Bible—in fact, not even allowed to read—they developed an alternate *hermeneutic* (method for interpreting a text or context) based on memory and analysis of their own situation. They remembered that Jesus set people free, so why were they in bondage? They remembered the stories of the Exodus from slavery to freedom, so where was God for them? They remembered the God of love, so why did they feel the lash?

Those memories coupled with their lived experience proved to be a powerful mixture, which was harbored in the spirituals that often carried messages not really understood by the slaveholders. For example, "Steal Away to Jesus" originally announced the night meetings that slaves held. In those meetings the alternate gospel was discussed—the one that spoke of freedom and dignity. The meetings were necessary because many white preachers who worked with slaves were selective in the material that they used for homilies. The slaves were made familiar with the story of Ham and the Levitical codes that support human bondage (Lev. 25:44–46). They had heard the Pauline writings that extolled slaves, "Slaves show obedience to your masters in the flesh with fear and trembling, in simplicity of heart as to Christ" (Eph. 6:5).

The liberating Christ was kept a well-guarded secret. A white Christ was preached instead, and slaves when baptized had to declare that the freedom of baptism was from sin and not from slavery. This white Christ—supposedly a friend of black people—was an oppressor. Therefore, the unofficial and dangerous slave gatherings offered new understandings; the black Christ began to emerge.

The slaves easily identified with the suffering of Jesus, and they took it to mean that he would understand their needs and act for them. It was not unusual to find that Jesus had been re-imaged as a second Moses who would come and lead his people to freedom out of their dire situations. The Christ they fashioned in their clandestine meetings was One who sided with God's actions in freeing Daniel and Jonah and would soon be acting on behalf of the new Jonahs, Daniels, and Israelites. This belief gave the communities a sense of hope—and individuals the feeling of self-worth that God would see them as worthy of God's intervention.

The white Christ did not foster a need for social justice. But the white Christ was slowly being replaced by the black Christ, who was the champion of freedom and solidarity with oppressed persons. As early as 1829 Robert Alexander Young was calling Christ black and declaring that God would send a Messiah born of a black woman to set God's people free.[5] Others stressed that it was necessary for black self-esteem to be able to think of Christ as black, whatever Christ's actual color might have been.

Marcus Garvey was the first to suggest that Jesus of Nazareth was actually black, claiming that he was from the tribe of Jesse, which was known to have African blood.[6] Thus, he had a special relationship with black people that was cemented by the black man, Simon of Cyrene, carrying his cross.

The Civil Rights Movement

The early attempts at identity and self-esteem beyond slavery did not fully emerge as a potent force until the civil rights movement of the 1960s. At that time black consciousness was raised, and people were keen to make explicit their African heritage. The white Christ, however, was still lurking in the background as a weapon used by those who wished to keep the social order untouched. The two dominant figures during the time of the civil rights movement were Martin Luther King and Malcolm X. They differed in approach from each other.

Malcolm X observed that the worship of a white deity, however liberative, was unhealthy for the black psyche. He asserted that at best such worship led to internalized racism on behalf of the black community. Black people had to liberate themselves from anything to do with the white devils, and that included the white Christ. That Christ allowed people to express themselves in worship once a week but kept them without a voice in the everyday affairs of their lives. That Christ called people to believe but not to act for justice. That Christ could have no place in the new consciousness of black people. That Christ kept people enslaved to white racist culture. Instead black people need self-love, self-defense, and black independence, and any means necessary could be used to achieve justice.

King, in contrast, emphasized the liberating God of Exodus who would change the lives of black people by demanding justice and freedom. King's religion spoke of love for all humanity, an integrated society, and redemptive suffering. King was totally against using violence. He encouraged his followers to stand fast when fire hoses or dogs were unleashed against them so that the actions of the oppressors could be seen as violence.[7]

Other leaders also figure into the development of black theology. Albert Cleague, for example, pointed out that Mary was of the tribe of

Judah, which had black races mixed in with it, so she gave birth to a black son. He suggested that Jesus had African blood and was related to black Americans. His motivation was similar to Malcolm's—black people could not build dignity on their knees in front of a white Christ.

Still others developed a different image of the black Christ. J. Deotis Roberts used black to emphasize the universal nature of Christ. Black people have as much right as any to imagine Christ in their image. He was aware of the pride that black people could gain from assuming that divine incarnation could be black, but he also warned against trapping Christ in black culture, a point subsequently explored by womanist theologians.[8]

James Cone's Black Liberation Christology

James Cone used the notion of the blackness of Christ, in spite of the reservations of some, to show that Jesus identified with oppressed persons. Cone emphasized that in a white racist society black people are oppressed; therefore, it is accurate to say that Jesus is black. He wanted theologians to face the issue of race in the United States. He wrote his book *Black Theology and Black Power* in a provocative tone. Some theologians dismissed it as an emotive outburst with no serious content. But they missed his point: Western theological discourse is white, it is based on white concepts, and it promotes a white Christ.

Cone is interested in finding a theological discourse rooted in the person of Jesus that is relevant to the black experience. He believes that it is necessary to find some evidence of the historical Jesus, or any attempt to apply the Christian message in everyday black reality is built on air. But if whites have made Jesus in their own image, is not this move to a black Christ the same? Cone warns against making Jesus in one's own image as whites have done. He encourages the placing of Jesus as the oppressed One whose earthly life was with the oppressed of the world. Unless the oppressed of today can know that Jesus the man was caught up in the same battles that they are involved in, he gives them no real hope, but merely a metaphysical dream.

Cone's Christology, therefore, is rooted in establishing that Jesus was the oppressed One. He demonstrates how even Jesus' birth placed him with the dispossessed and outcasts. He was born in a stable, which Cone equates with a beer case in a ghetto alley.[9] Even though Cone is not claiming factual accuracy for the birth narratives, he is claiming that they have deep theological significance. Yet some objections can be raised. First, there was no room in the inn because of excessive demand at the time. Joseph and Mary would at other times have had access to the inn, a privilege that many blacks have been denied in the United States. Second, a stable is not really the same as a ghetto alley; it is warm and protected from the elements and has access to the main building should further provisions be required. After all the innkeeper had not turned them away altogether but offered alternate (but poorer) accommodations. Thus, as an illustration of powerlessness and dispossession, this may not be the best one. Jesus' family had a home to go to, and his father had a trade to practice in order to keep his family fed. Is this the case for those living in a beer case in the alley? Perhaps the most that can be said is that this son of an artisan chose to fight for and identify with the truly oppressed.

Cone presses his point and insists that Jesus' baptism and his temptations illustrate the degree to which he identified with poor people and sinners. Both show the meaning of God in the world: to be with the poor and to express a realm based on love, not judgment. Cone is annoyed by white scholastic attempts to explain away the emphasis placed on the poor by assuming the reference is to the poor in spirit. He condemns this as being a way of justifying their own privilege and preserving their white economic status. He ties this in with a white justification of enslavement, which he sees as a natural outcome of proclaiming no contradiction between wealth and the gospel.

There is no logical and absolute connection here, as his own situation shows. Cone is a privileged man, having taught at one of the finest educational institutions in the United States for more than twenty years and enjoying the palatial living that is connected with that school, but he would no doubt claim that he does not enslave anyone. He is making an absolutely fundamental point, that excessive wealth does disable large parts of society who work to generate it but do not profit from it, but he appears to be so concerned with making a racial point that he fails to make a necessary political point. Yes, Christendom has enslaved people, but so has Islam and so does Western secular and religious society in all its various shades. Are we to understand Cone's divisions between white and black as merely symbolic, that is, all who are poor may be seen as black, regardless of pigmentation, and all the rich as white? His rhetoric would lend itself to that understanding. Having said that, I agree with his main thesis that Jesus was intent on liberating humanity from inhumanity.[10]

For Cone, the death and resurrection of Jesus Christ are of crucial importance. In a sense they are at the center of his Christological thinking since they throw into relief the real essence of the life and ministry of Jesus. He says, "His death is the revelation of the freedom of God, taking upon himself the totality of human oppression; his resurrection is the disclosure that God is not defeated by oppression but transforms it into the possibility of freedom."[11] That is, those who are forced to live under oppressive regimes do not have to do so as though death were the end; they can live free of worry about economic insecurity and political tyranny. The freedom that Christ gives is freedom from the fear of death, and so the oppressed can stand against the oppressors. They are free to revolt.

By focusing on the historical Jesus, Cone emphasized the importance of history as the foundation for Christology. The meaning of Jesus is an existential question since we know best who he is when we too suffer oppression and have to decide how to resist or whether to collude. Jesus is black because the black community in the United States suffers oppression simply because of its blackness. Cone contends that if Jesus Christ is not black, then his resurrection has no significance for the black community. He also vehemently resists all attempts by white theologians to suggest that oppression is found in all kinds of communities, not just the black ones. Cone states, "Any statement about Jesus today that fails to consider blackness as the decisive factor about his person is a denial of the New Testament message. . . . Jesus Christ must be black so that blacks can know that their liberation is his liberation."[12]

The definition of Christ as black represents total opposition to white values and culture. The black Christ names as good all that the white Christ has named as evil or has ignored as irrelevant in the liberation struggle. Cone believes that the empowerment gained from this subversion will enable the black community to rise up against its oppressors. He acknowledges that it will be difficult for whites to accept the whiteness of existence, in other words, the way the world is constructed toward whiteness. It is his hope that the black Christ will throw this into relief for them. Cone says that the literal color of Jesus is not important, but the blackness of Christ is crucial. By proclaiming such a message, we are translating first-century symbols into ones that are relevant for today, Christ took the misery of the world on the Divine Self, and today that means Christ took on blackness.[13]

For Cone, the realm of God arises when black people refuse to be defined by white values and take hold of a quality in their existence that has previously been denied or at least conspired against by the white system. God's realm comes when black people no longer need white approval so that living does not actually require that they sacrifice or destroy something of themselves. Whites will not see this realm coming, but we are reminded that not all recognize the Messiah, so this is to be expected. This realm will not be of the purely spiritual order that Cone claims is so often used to keep social systems in place.[14] It will be an actualized affair, visibly removing the oppression of whiteness from the shoulders of all who have suffered it. The black Christ brings this realm into being through instilling pride, self-worth, and resurrection hope into the oppressed.

There has been some criticism of black theology, not least in relation to the ambivalent meaning that black often carries in this context. For some theologians, Christ is literally black while for others the blackness is a matter of identification with the oppressed. There is a problem in both cases: Jesus was not black, nor was he pristinely white, as he is portrayed in much religious art. Further, by assuming black to mean the poor and oppressed, one creates a difficult situation for blacks who are neither poor nor oppressed. Where is their liberative model to come from? Cone would no doubt argue that even he, in his position of privilege, is still systemically oppressed. However, there is a danger of falling into purely victim mode, and that would be regrettable. Certainly, he is correct in asserting that the world is constructed around whiteness, and this has to be challenged, but there is a danger in sanctifying all that comes out of black communities. Not everything in the black culture is affirming and positive for black people, and there is also much black-on-black oppression. By claiming that all evil springs from whiteness, there is a risk that other evils will go unchallenged. Cone runs the risk of becoming outdated through failing to answer a fundamental question amidst new black affluence. The question is, How should black Americans live to keep from oppressing their black cousins around the world? In such an advanced capitalist society as the United States, even when the wealth is black wealth, it still hurts others. Black theology needs to urgently address this crushing reality.

WOMANIST LIBERATION CHRISTOLOGIES

Womanist theologians are pointing out that by exclusively concentrating on race, black theologians have overlooked the crucial elements in any liberative struggle, those of class, gender, and sexual orientation. Cone recognized that he did not address the role of women in the black struggles, and he has attempted to make amends, but some feel it is too little, too late. Just as in the black power movement, the liberation of black men set the agenda in black theology. In the early days of the struggle, many black women did not wish to deflect attention from what they also perceived as the central issue, black power. They were anxious that if the black community appeared divided by sexism, the whole liberation movement would be discredited.

However, the womanist movement realizes and proclaims that black women are in double jeopardy, at least, since they are oppressed members of an oppressed group. They may be in triple jeopardy if they are also poor, as is the case for many. This realization has caused womanists to search for a politics of wholeness, which has led them to criticize the haves both inside and outside the black community. Those within the black community are understood as sustaining a white way of life, which is harmful to their poorer black sisters and brothers. The commitment to wholeness has also led womanists to challenge heterosexism, which has often been rife in black theology and black churches where homosexuality has been thought of as a white disease. The womanist movement challenges both the sexism of black theology and the racism of feminist theology. Recently, due to its commitment to a politics of wholeness, it has sought to do this by siding with the oppressed of color from around the world. This work is mostly done through EATWOT and is a concrete expression of the theory that no woman is free until all women are free. Therefore to a certain extent, womanists are beginning to address issues of global oppression that their brothers failed to grasp.

Womanists who have done the most explicit work on Christology are Jacquelyn Grant and Kelly Brown Douglas. Naturally, any womanist appreciation of Christ begins with a recognition of the many-layered oppression under which black women labor, coupled with a determination to break free. There is also a double-edged approach to black culture from a womanist perspective—women are more critical of it than the men tended to be. While praising and valuing the parts that are liberating and affirming, womanists are aware that some parts are destructive. Douglas gives the example of rap music, which is an important part of black youth identity but also contains many negative aspects, such as images of violence to women.[15] Rap is not to be taken uncritically and lauded as black identity and therefore as above suspicion.

Each so-called authentic black experience has to be measured against the vision of wholeness that womanism holds out for the community. Underpinning this vision is the firm knowledge that all are created as valued and loved creatures in the sight of God. All, therefore, have to affirm this by the way they act toward one another within the community. Christ is active in the black community by calling it to rid itself of anything that is divisive or oppressive.[16] This is true in the religious realm as much as in the secular. Douglas tells us: "In regard to Black religion, a religio-cultural analysis challenges any aspect of Black faith that perpetuates the discrimination of particular segments of the Black community. For instance, the ways in which the Black church uses the Bible in the oppression of women, gays and lesbians will be confronted."[17]

Womanists are able to define the black Christ as female as well as male. Anyone who works for the community to free it from external and internal slavery and oppression can be seen as the face of Christ. Therefore, Harriet Tubman or Sojourner Truth may reflect the face of the black female Christ.[18] This highlights a number of things about Christ in womanist thought. Christ is performative; what Christ did and what others do in following Christ are more important than who Christ was in a metaphysical sense. People are called to action rather than simple declarations of faith. Actions aimed at creating wholeness are those that are most liberating. Further, Christ the judge is present in the faces of the most disadvantaged black women who call others to continual accountability.[19]

The emphasis on wholeness and life-affirming action presents problems for womanist theologians when they consider traditional models of atonement. The notion that Jesus died for us is not a healthy paradigm in a community in which coercion and suffering for the benefit of others have been harsh and lived realities. Douglas is not alone in declaring that a new understanding of this central doctrine has to be sought.[20] She is also fully aware that many within the black community find it strangely comforting to be able to identify with the suffering of Christ and to feel that Christ saw, and sees, theirs. However, Douglas reminds us that black people in slavery who declared that Jesus Christ was their liberator knew nothing of Nicene Creeds. Their declaration was firmly based in the reality of the here and now and not metaphysical theology. What they believed Jesus Christ could do for them in the dire reality of everyday life was the crucial thing. This Christ, then, was not One to be set aside for worship but was in the nitty-gritty of life, and the transformative power of following Christ's actions was emphasized. Womanists have developed an understanding of Christ that can never move far from the realities of the lives of ordinary black women.[21]

While many womanists make a connection between Jesus' suffering and that of women, they are keen not to let his suffering obscure theirs. Alice Walker places a plea in the mouth of one of her characters, Tashi, that the suffering of women should be the focus of sermons rather than the long-ago suffering of Jesus. Tashi asks, "Was woman herself not the tree of life? And was she not crucified? Not in some age no one remembers, but right now, daily, in many lands."[22] This point requires a major shift in the Christian understanding of suffering. Delores Williams[23] challenges the notions of surrogacy and structural domination innate in traditional interpretations. Jesus is released to glory by his suffering while black women are imprisoned in theirs, yet encouraged to believe that suffering is somehow sacred. In identifying women with the tree of life, crucified, womanists are careful not to glorify this identification. Rather, they look for the end of suffering and the full flourishing of their lives in this world. Christ, then, is the healer and the One who releases others into abundant life.

Douglas, although a womanist, does not exclude men from the liberating and prophetic actions of Christ within the community. Grant, on the other hand, tends to emphasize the liberating activity of women. Like Cone and the others, Grant places her theology against a background of slavery and the accompanying oppressions. She holds onto this history when starting her theology from women's experience. She insists that the experiences of white and black women cannot be viewed as the same not simply because of contemporary differences but also because of their history. It is a history in which white women, although oppressed, were also the oppressors. This phenomenon has not died out, and according to Grant, feminist theology is white and racist. It has used the tools of white scholarship, the resources of white culture, and overlooked the deep divide created by the years of slavery when white and black women were not sisters in the struggle for freedom. She tells us:

> To say that many Black women are suspicious of the feminist movement, then, is to speak mildly about their responses to it. Put succinctly, women of the dominant culture are perceived as the enemy. Like their social, sexual and political White male partners, they have as their primary goal the suppression, if not oppression, of the Black race and the advancement of the dominant culture. Because of this perception, many believe that Black feminism is a contradiction in terms.[24]

Despite this apparently unbridgeable gulf, black women are employing many of the tools of feminist analysis in their theological work. Most are clear that by starting from black experience, the discourse becomes womanist and not feminist. This distinction is now widely honored if at first it was somewhat misunderstood. This is an African American designation and not one that travels easily, for example, to Britain. The historical background is different and the construction of racism has also been different, and so it has to be argued that there is little commonality of experience.

Grant maintains that black women do their theology out of a tridimensional oppression, that of class, race, and gender. As a result of their gender and their race, they make up a disproportionate number of the poor.[25] Grant is correct that any attempt at a theology of liberation has to take all these elements into account. As with all liberation theologies, womanists are very careful when it comes to the use of the Bible. They use it, but they interpret it from the lives of the people rather than placing layers of dominant interpretation onto their lives. Through the pages of the Bible and reflection on their lives, womanists have found Jesus, God incarnate, who signifies freedom. This freedom is the kind brought by a political messiah[26] and not simply a spiritual enlightener. Along with Cone and others, Grant sees Christ as black as a necessary step in understanding what this political liberation would look like. Christ identified as a black woman places the Divine among the most deprived and places a resurrection hope in the midst of despair.

Further, the black female Christ begins to destabilize much of the imagery that has played a negative part in the lives of women. It is possible to begin to understand that the humanity of Jesus gave him power and not his maleness alone. This in turn calls for a reexamination of women as representatives of Eve and therefore their lack of ability to represent the Divine. In claiming the humanity of Christ as their own, black women are becoming subjects in their new and unfolding discourse rather than being objectified in the discourse of others. This new subjectivity does not actually make the womanist position totally exclusivist. Grant argues that there is an acknowledged universalism at the heart of womanist Christology. The same Christ who works with black women as they fight their tridimensional oppression is also in the race struggle with black men, the sexism struggle with all women, and the poverty struggle with blacks and whites alike.[27]

In finding their particularity, black women also find the universally liberating Christ. Although Grant does not explicitly mention it, this understanding of the universality of Christ enables the black/white nature of Christ to be expanded into ethnicity. It has sometimes seemed to observers of black theology that black theologians view the world as simply divided into black and white, underprivilege belonging to black skins and obscene wealth and privilege to white skins. This is a rather gross generalization—and one that was never really a true reflection of the discourse. However, there has not been an explicit acknowledgment of the gradations of color (by this I do not mean light and dark skin alone but ethnicity). For example, the Irish, who are often very pale skinned, have suffered, and do suffer, under a great deal of ethnic prejudice in Britain. The Cretans under Ottoman rule suffered greatly as do the Tibetans under the Chinese. In other words, color is not just black and white, and prejudice and oppression are not always from the lighter to the darker skins.

Black theology and womanist theology destroy any illusion of there being good masters, and they expose the abusive use of the Bible in earlier attempts to create these good masters. These theologies have turned the use of the Bible into a powerful tool of self-affirmation and prophetic liberation. The God of the Exodus and the black Christ of freedom liberate people from the mind-set of oppression and help them to realize that oppression is not the result of cosmic forces or the result of sin. Oppression is always built into a system and, as such, can always be dismantled. The liberating black Christ calls people to believe that they deserve to be free and that they have the power to achieve that freedom. The black Christ, above all else, encourages black self-love in a world that encourages self-hatred and self-denial. From this love and self-affirmation comes the power to resist all that would crush black personhood.

IN BRITAIN, JESUS IS DREAD

The black community in Britain is largely from the Caribbean, and the majority entered Britain in the 1950s and 1960s at the invitation of the government. Much older and established black communities in Britain had been in the country for two hundred years or more. Their origins were mixed but largely connected with seaports and the supporting industries. In other words, very few of the black population in Britain descend from those who entered the country on slave ships. However, slavery lurks in the Caribbean background and casts its shadow over the development of black British theology. There was an interesting mix of African and European religion during the time of slavery, which went largely unchecked due to the limited amount of missionary work in the Caribbean. For example, in Jamaica there was no missionary work for the first 150 years of plantation history.[28] Aspects of African religion could find a place in, and adapt, Christianity. The Creator God who could be either male or female and was immanent in the world was a huge influence, as was the veneration of ancestors, which gave a sense of community that in turn gave meaning to individual lives.[29] Although these aspects influenced Christianity, they also remained intact in other traditions that were never affected by Christianity and therefore provided a distinct cultural influence.

When Caribbean Christians entered Britain, they did not always enjoy a warm welcome in the churches. Even if they did, they found the culture of the churches far removed from their own, the use of language imaged evil as black, and the very restricted expression of worship did not suit many black people. With the establishment of black churches worship was free to be fully embodied and black. For the second generation of black Christians in Britain the concern has moved on from finding a safe and empowering place to worship to showing that "black culture contains a prophetic and spiritual dimension."[30] Their task is to materialize an alternate social reality in which blackness is powerful. As in the United States the atmosphere of oppression is not purely external. The black churches in Britain are oppressive in matters of sexuality and gender. Therefore, the black Christ in this context, as in others, has to critique the community from which the black Christ emerges as much as the dominant community.

Black theology is a relatively new discipline in Britain and can be expected to take its lead from the work done in the United States. The central thesis—that black theologians must engage in the creation of images of Jesus that lead to sociopolitical wholeness—is lifted from Kelly Brown Douglas.[31] However, the work of Robert Beckford gives this general thesis a very particular slant, which is sexual wholeness. He argues that representations of black sexuality have for centuries been at the service of colonial and imperialistic needs. The myths that surround it have excused sexual exploitation of the black races and added fuel to the rationale for slavery. The logic is perverse: black people are sex-crazy animals and want it with anyone, a myth that white men have perpetuated with dire consequences. On the other hand, it is the responsibility of the civilized and sexually restrained white races to control the black beast, particularly to protect white female virtue. Black bodies, while being exploited, were also represented as evil and sexually dangerous in Christian art and white popular culture. Beckford is saddened by the fact that some black youth culture expands these stereotypes, believing that it is portraying blacks positively. He argues that what is being reproduced is an "internalized and reproduced Eurocentric representation."[32] The rampant, aggressive macho sexuality that is being celebrated is actually a threat to the black community since it alienates black women and black gays and lesbians and ultimately fails to challenge racism. The black sexual Christ has to engage with these negative stereotypes in pursuit of communal wholeness.

Jesus is Dread for black people in Britain; that is, he symbolizes freedom, power, and fulfillment. Therefore, he has to be Dread in relation to the dysfunctional images of sexuality that deny full humanity to black people.[33] The fully incarnate Christ must liberate black people from the dehumanization that representations of their sexuality have brought about. The first step is to sexualize Christ. After all, it is the desexualized Christ who makes others of those who are sexually active, let alone stereotyped through their sexuality. Creating an icon of a black, sexed Christ, such as the *Lion of Judah* depicting him as a Masai warrior whose genitalia are obvious through his garments, is one way in which to address the problem. This icon shows a very dignified and unthreatening, even gentle, figure who is obviously a male. Its purpose is to highlight that sexuality is an innate part of our humanness but is not the overriding, defining factor, especially if such definitions are going to lead to exclusion and prejudice.

Beckford is anxious that the sexed Christ should be an icon of freedom for all and not just the black, male, heterosexual community. He wants a voice to be given to black gays and lesbians,[34] who have a particularly difficult time in a racist, homophobic society. Beckford acknowledges that the support they would usually get from the black community to stand against racism is often withdrawn because of their sexual orientation. He feels that the image of a sexed warrior Christ signals that the whole community has to fight for the rights of each person within it. If the black community dehumanizes part of itself because of preference, it plays into the hands of racist stereotyping, which would dehumanize it all on the grounds of sexuality. In short, the black community cannot require from outside what it is not willing to grant within the community.

Jesus as Dread demands that all structures of oppression are destroyed, and that includes those set in place by black people themselves. This concept also acknowledges that blackness is not homogeneous, and so Dread fights for progress through diversity. There is no desire to impose a uniform blackness on blacks in Britain; that is being fought against. Celebration of diversity is a very strong theme in the emerging womanist discourse in Britain. Black women have been simultaneously central in churches and marginalized in leadership. They also feel that the feminist theological movement in Britain has ignored them. This, like the debate in the United States, depends on one's vantage point. Serious attempts have been made to include black women in theological conferences, but they have met with limited responses.[35] The problem seems to be one of theological language and approach, much of which is seen as irrelevant for black women. Work is being done by black women to see Jesus through Afrocentric eyes and to access how this awakened vision of Jesus will affect women's position in the church. The feminist community in Britain needs just such input as does the black male community. Both will be called to repentance and new ways of partnership when this new agenda finally emerges.

BLACK AND AFRICAN THEOLOGY

Theology that emanates from Africa is contextually different from that found among African Americans and among blacks in Britain. Further, due to the varying contexts found in Africa, there is a range of thought that is almost too vast to cover. For example, the understanding of Christ developed under apartheid in South Africa will be different from that emerging among Ghanaian women. The cultural diversity of the region we so conveniently call Africa is immense and creates many pictures of Christ.

A central question in African theology is that of the relationship between the indigenous culture and the colonial impact of Christianity. Some of the earliest forms of Christianity survive in small areas of Africa while the rest of the Christianity that is evident comes from the missionary activities that took place from the sixteenth century onward. Christianity did not come alone, and what we know as different African states are the result of the carving up of the continent by the intrepid explorers and the governments they represented. The result of colonizing activity is a discrediting and undervaluing of all that is indigenous and replacing it, or at the very least overlaying it, with the superior culture one is importing. Africa was not immune to this and suffered from having its culture castigated and Christianity imported wholesale. The rearrangement of society that took place under colonization had, as it always does, bad effects on Africa. Families were often broken up so that the women could serve in the white houses while the men remained in the fields or the mines. In South Africa the men were deported to work in mines thousands of miles away from their families. The economic structure that had relied largely on agriculture became altered to fit Western demands and not the needs of the indigenous people—the results of which have been famine and death. Any education that was offered to the people followed Western patterns. The absurdity is evident if we consider African children reading Shakespeare in huts in rural areas. How useful could it ever be imagined such study would be? Traditional family patterns were disrupted, and insistence on monogamy, for example, often led to the deaths of women or their descent into prostitution.

From 1958 to 1965 the colonizers—the British, French, and Belgians—withdrew from Africa but tried to ensure that those who took power would be sympathetic to neocolonial control. This anxiety about where power would lie was over resources and their continued cheap availability for the West, not a paternal concern about the conditions of the African population. This withdrawal process was met with conflict, which led to suffering on behalf of the indigenous peoples. South Africa, with the largest white population, took the longest to find independence from apartheid, and despite the political freedoms, many of the legacies of that regime live on. This is most clearly visible in the enormous gap between the wealthy white elite and the poor black masses. There is also the huge scar of oppression to be dealt with. The Truth and Reconciliation Committee has a sensitive and complicated task to carry out if justice is to underpin freedom.

Two major forms of theology have emerged in Africa since the 1960s: African theology and black theology. The former took shape under the guidance of religious anthropologists, such as John Mbiti and E. Bojaji Idowu, who were concerned with the inculturation of Christian theology into the African context. The latter was influenced by the movements in the United States, and consciousness-raising was concerned with liberation, not inculturation. African theology raises many questions, such as, Is there only one African culture, and how does one find it under the layers of colonization? This is an ongoing process with women now joining the debate and asking that their culture also be included in what is called African. There is a growing optimism that African culture can be rescued, not simply invented, and that once this occurs, the ancient spiritual values will reemerge and be seen as compatible with biblical values. This allows for an integration of Christianity into the African worldview rather than a denial of indigenous culture and imposition of foreign thought forms. The result will face Christianity with many new questions.

Anthropology and cosmology are both seen in a positive light and are quite unlike traditional Christian understandings. It is impossible, in the African mind, to separate the salvation of human beings from that of the universe. This understanding has Christological implications in that the incarnation becomes something more than a merely human birth. The Christ is viewed as clothed in the whole cosmos in the act of incarnation. This inclusive view is totally in keeping with the African understanding of community, which encompasses the whole person. The individual is not a differentiated human person but interpersonal and cosmic relations combined in a skin.[36] The person is not seen in individualistic terms, as in the West, and it is acknowledged that each person exists only because all people exist and the cosmos exists. This mutually empowering connection extends beyond the grave, and those who are no longer living are understood to play a vital role in the continued well-being of the living. Striking similarities are thought to exist between the African worldview and that found in the Hebrew Scriptures. The sense of corporate personality and the affinity with the land run through veins divided by thousands of years and miles. For the African, the land is not something that is owned but something that gives identity; it roots individuals in the corporate self, both living and dead. The lament of the psalmist, "How shall we sing the Lord's song in a strange land?" (Ps. 137:4) speaks to the soul of the African who is fighting for land rights. By acknowledging the similarities between the Hebrew Scriptures and their own heritage, African theologians are actually critiquing Christianity. This critique goes to the heart attacking individualism, dualism, and colonialism, the latter being underpinned by the notion of a universal gospel.

The universally encompassing nature of Christ is understood distinctly by African theologians. Far from making it necessary to go out and preach the gospel from one's own cultural perspective, the appearance of the Christ illustrates that God has always been present in one's own history and culture. It is possible to make this claim only if one understands the interrelatedness of all life, which suggests that the Christ could not appear if the time was not universally right. Some African theologians would not agree with this scheme, claiming that the whole concept of the Christ, even before its dualistic overlays, is foreign to African culture. That an individual alone should have such a universal influence does not sit well with the African mind. They claim that the missionary process has been so successful, it has even caused a false remembering of heritage and culture.

Despite these expressed reservations, African theology has been accused, mainly by black theologians, of working within such a tight Christian framework that it overlooks matters of exploitation and the need for liberation. That was a fair criticism in the early days, but as can be seen in the declaration that came from the Pan African Conference of Third World Theologians in 1977, it has awakened to the need for a liberative eye. The declaration clearly showed that African theology understood oppression to be political as well as cultural and that certain aspects of culture may be oppressive to certain sectors of society, for example, women.[37] As I have already mentioned, the whole notion of culture is problematic. African theology has often been criticized for seeing culture in too static a way and not recognizing that many of the aspects that allow Christianity its solid footing are now changing in secular African culture. The debate over the nature of culture is an ever expanding one, and all that can really be hoped for is that African theology will be aware of the process and not try to resurrect a fossil.

There is a very real sense in which becoming Christian in Africa is a taking on of the life of Jesus Christ in the hope of finding ways to overcome the multiple oppressions that are rife in that society. So

Christ is not just the One who assures Africans that their ancient traditions had God within them but is also the One who gives them hope for the future from within their own culture. Christ is the figure who helps them regain confidence and pride in their own heritage. This is a far cry from the Christ of the colonizing powers who attempted to crush cultures under Western, dualistic, universal feet and is yet another indication that the spirit of people will not be chained even in the name of the Divine.

Black theology with its emphasis on liberation was, unsurprisingly, developed in South Africa during the time of the antiapartheid struggles. Persons involved in the forefront of the movement such as Desmond Tutu, Allan Boesak, and Itumeleng Mosala were concerned to develop a theology free from any colonial hint, one that was strong enough to throw off the racist system under which they toiled. From the beginning it was clear that "it is not merely people who need to be liberated. The gospel, so abused and exploited, also needs to be liberated."[38] It needed to be liberated because as things stood, there was no good news for black people under apartheid. To be black in South Africa was not to naturally experience the goodness of creation or the love and mercy believed to be part of the Christian message. There was a severe mismatch between the Word and the acts. Under the everyday situation experienced by black South Africans, to ask them to love themselves was tantamount to a revolution since such self-love necessitated the overthrow of the oppressive regime. Boesak combines the notions of self-love and the power to be and says, "The power to be, the courage to affirm one's own human dignity, must inevitably lead to the transformation of structures to fulfill its search for completion and wholeness."[39]

Affirming oneself as made in the image of God also emphasizes that divine power, granted by God, works in us. The sharing of this power makes us fully human and illustrates in practice the Christian message demonstrated by Jesus. For Boesak, black power is having the courage to be black in a white world. That is to say, having the courage to value and celebrate a black way of being, to declare it is as valid as the white way, to reclaim blackness as valuable in the sight of God, and to give up aspiring to white values, even if they could be achieved.[40] Boesak and others relied heavily on the work of Martin Luther King and James Cone in their own explorations into the radical nature of daring to be black.

This daring has the power to shake Christian foundations. For example, M. M. Thomas suggested that even a concept like the reign of God cannot be identified with the church since that institution has too often been white and oppressive. Rather, when one dares to be black, it encourages revolutionary ferment, which signals the power and promise of Christ. It is only revolution in oppressive regimes that leads to a fuller and richer life for the oppressed. The promises of Christ are inescapably linked with new discoveries of selfhood and the desire for freedom accompanying it. Thomas does not reduce Christ to a revolution but states that when Christ is linked with revolution, it becomes more human and geared toward a new humanity.[41] For Thomas, Christ is revealing new ways to the people of Africa through revolution and the creative possibilities that can open up in that way. Christ working through historical events will produce ultimate victory because Christ is the Risen One. This is not to deny that there are evil forces also at work, but they will not triumph. The question that springs to mind is, What about those who are drowned in the raging torrent of revolution? The answer has to be that God had no pity on the Egyptians, so why should Boers fare any better? The power of Christ in these situations pushes always toward humanization, and where there is resistance to this, it pushes aside that resistance. There is no guarantee that only the oppressors will perish if they resist change. Revolutions are bloody; however, the follower of Christ is the one who is "defined by imaginative and behavioral sensitivity to what God is doing in the world to make and to keep human life, human."[42]

The South African government realized the power of such rhetoric and banned it. The government prohibited the publication of materials and followed up by carrying out many house arrests. Black theology was seen as being the theological wing of black power, which in turn was understood as promoting Marxist revolution.[43] This condemnation was similar to that made against Latin American theology, one based on negative propaganda rather than fact. Black theology placed greater emphasis on biblical theology and faith than even Latin American theologians did. For people such as Boesak and Tutu the kind of reconciliation that is required can be found only through faith since it is in Christ that both reconciliation and liberation occur. The fact that revenge has not appeared to be the overriding factor in the politics of the new South Africa says a great deal for those who have for too long been cruelly treated. Reconciliation requires justice, and this lies at the heart of the process in South Africa. Black theology still has a vital role to play in bringing the experiences of people to light and placing them at the heart of both politics and theology. Apartheid may be over, but economic oppression is not. The Christ who demanded revolution based on self-love and affirmation now demands that the emerging society acts as a liberating force throughout the world. In its own push for economic justice it has to be careful not to place a foot on the neck of other countries struggling for survival. Because of the grip of global capitalism, this is a daunting task. However, whatever it takes, the newly freed must not become the oppressors.

Both black theology and African theology have their critics. Indeed, they criticize each other, usually on the basis of their respective emphases. Black theologians think that African theologians do not have a sufficient understanding of the fluidity of culture, while African theologians believe that their counterparts are uncritically importing U.S. theology. Both groups now seem to agree that liberation and inculturation are necessary in their context, and so there is more working together than there is disagreement. Some Western liberation theologians are also anxious about the conservative views held regarding women and sexuality that are emerging from Africa. Many African bishops are the most vehemently antigay and antifeminist, and this view seems as rooted in their culture as it does in their Christianity.

The Will to Arise

Not surprisingly, both groups had managed to forget women in the debates, and so emerging black feminist theology is calling them to task for the omission. A significant group of feminist theologians are scattered throughout Africa, and the most well known in the West is probably Mercy Amba Oduyoye. These women are involved in the work of cultural critique, which is no simple matter considering the diverse cultures in Africa. This critique encompasses traditional African cultures, Christianity, and Western imperialism from a woman's perspective. In this way women are claiming the right to decide what is a positive cultural influence in their lives and what is not. By approaching both culture and religion in this way, they can be said to be bridging the gap between African and liberation theologies. They are not reverencing culture to the point of sacrificing themselves to it nor are they abandoning culture in the hope of liberation.

The African woman is often viewed as powerful within her culture, but this does not always lead to a powerful role in society. Her power is also seen as making her dangerous; therefore, many regulations are placed on women to keep feminine evil at bay. Through these restrictions, the power of women is placed at the service of men, which is not an unusual story under patriarchy. Myths about women's power invariably suggest that once women serve men, their potential threat is neutralized. Africa, like other patriarchal countries, values strength in women only when it is harnessed to the furtherance of male privilege. African women theologians are striving for female power to be celebrated for its own sake and used in the service of women's needs.

The picture is not all gloom, and African theologians, while challenging negative customs, are also reclaiming some of the more positive aspects. These include stories of female deities, leaders, and life enhancers. Far from uncritically accepting that Christianity liberated women from the oppressions of African society, the women are examining the negative role of Christianity in women's lives, especially when joined with colonialism. Although such a combination has had a negative influence on all Africans, the way in which it has affected women was distinct. They lost what political and economic power they had and suffered under not only a racist regime but also a more patriarchal one. Christianity encouraged women to see the cross as a symbol that helped them bear their suffering rather than resist it.

A critique of this approach has caused women not to abandon Christianity altogether but to examine the ways in which Christ can liberate them within their culture. African feminist theologians have an immovable belief that Christ is on their side and will help them create just societies. There is, then, a tension in Christology since liberation lies both in the help of Christ now and in the future just society that will exist. Underpinning this is the knowledge that Jesus Christ is their personal friend who accepts them as they are and wishes to meet their needs in a personal way.[44] This Christological development highlights the extent to which women in the African context need such a friend and advocate, One who will touch and heal them spiritually and physically.

Jesus Christ is also viewed as the One who enfleshes the power of God and is able to share that power with followers.[45] The sharing of power is particularly relevant for women and other oppressed groups since this power is shared by all of Jesus Christ's followers, not just the elite. The power of Jesus Christ is often prophetic, and this means that there are a number of black Messiahs in the independent churches, that is, those who have embodied the prophetic nature of Christ. These prophetic voices are often raised in relation to social justice issues and lend a powerful impetus to the struggle for freedom.

Another aspect of Christ is important in the African search for a holistic Christology, and that is cosmological. Anne Nasimiyu-Wasike images Jesus Christ as the cosmological liberator,[46] the One who hears the groaning of nature, heals the pain, and overcomes the exploitation. Jesus Christ who calmed the storms in his own day can overcome the droughts, floods, and famines that are killing Africans today. Christ is the One who can restore balance to nature and in this way help the liberation of people. This very important element in the Christological debate has been overlooked for centuries by those who have been more comfortable with understanding universal balance as meaning that dominant values will prevail.

The point that Nasimiyu-Wasike highlights is a crucial one; liberation has as its basic component food. People have to be in control of their own sustenance. They must not be dependent for the very basics in life if they are to be seen as truly free. Africa tells a scandalous tale of Western intervention that has played a major part in the increase of drought and famine and the increased inability of Africans to cope with such conditions. The colonizer knew best about ways of farming, grazing, and crop rotation. Added to this the masters required that resources be used to sustain their wealth—not the population's survival. This combination of arrogance and greed has contributed in great measure to the ruination of many African economies. Much of the land is ruined, and many traditional, holistic ways of coping with the environment have been lost or are no longer up to the new tasks. There are also still colonial demands placed on Africa and its people, even if it is now called national debt. A cosmological Christology calls multinational companies to account and poses serious environmental questions. This Christ requires a major change in both the economy and the way in which industry operates and pollutes the cosmos. Africa, along with so many other countries, can no longer be used as a breeding ground for Western luxuries. Africa has to sit under its own vine with no demands from the West.

Just as Christ can heal the cosmos, Christ can heal people, and this is a very fundamental aspect of Christ in Africa. Many people who feel themselves empowered by Christ are healers and exorcists. There is a recognition that liberation can include both physical and mental health, just as much as empowering human relationships and cosmological freedom. Healing and exorcism have always been part of African religion, and a valuable contribution to theology as a whole is that we are being reminded of the holistic nature of both things. African feminist Christology provides us with an excellent holistic model. Nothing is too unimportant to be included and nothing is too grand to be outside the liberating power of Christ. While we may acknowledge that this seems in line with Jesus Christ, we have to admit that Christologies have often fallen short of this inclusivity. Jesus Christ, the imperial Sovereign of universal conquest, was not interested in cosmological health or for that matter the physical health of individuals, particularly the conquered. Indeed, Jesus Christ imaged as the Suffering Servant would positively have encouraged suffering in the service of imperial values. We should not underestimate the power of the Christ who is emerging from Africa. The demands of this pluralist, complex society will undoubtedly change the face of Christ, and it is to be hoped that this will be celebrated rather than seen with suspicion and knocked into line by those who still hold imperial power, albeit clothed as spiritual leadership.

Feminist theologians in Africa are aware that the challenge they bring is one that will have deep significance for the future. Therese Souga perceives that the challenge follows the example of women, mostly unnamed, in the Gospels. The Syro-Phoenician woman (Matt. 15:21–28) and the woman with the hemorrhage (Matt. 9:18–22) are very concrete examples of how ill-conceived stereotypes of women, even those held by Jesus, have to be faced, challenged, and overcome. The women were not only persistent, but they questioned how they were viewed by society and they made known their own reality (even if they have remained nameless for their trouble). Souga believes that African women are challenging the negative stereotypes that persist about them in the African church in the same way that those fore-mothers in faith did.[47] She concludes that they too will receive the healing that those women demanded. It is, however, a healing that is dispensed by Jesus, and she does not emphasize the role of the women in bringing about their healing except through their persistence. With Western eyes it would seem that more could be made of the Christlike actions of the Gospel women themselves, not only in their challenge of the oppressive systems that kept them restricted and prevented their access to healing. Nonetheless, those foremothers are seen as models for the active participation of African women in overcoming their cultural oppression. Mary, the mother of Jesus, is also a powerful symbol for many African women. Through giving birth to the Child of God, she is argued to have raised the status of childbearing, an activity for which African women have received very little credit despite its being seen as their purpose in life. Mary is a channel for them to claim more dignity and importance for one of their main tasks, that of bearing and raising children.

Christ, who entered Africa as a conqueror speaking white male language, is in the hands of women becoming a welcome guest who feels more at home in the culture. In addition, Christ is able to critique the culture not, as previously, with Western imperialist values, but with liberative praxis. "Christ is the true Human, the one who makes it possible for all persons to reach fulfillment and to overcome the historic alienations weighing them down."[48]

For African women, real Christology is performed each day as they struggle against the multifaceted oppressions facing them. This struggle is fueled by an unshakable belief that Christ and Christ's followers changed history. This Christ will shake the West much more than Constantine's conquering hero Christ.

It has been possible to concentrate in this chapter only on the main aspects of African American, womanist, black, and African theology. These areas are expanding and developing their discourse at a rapid rate. What emerges from this overview is a Christ who looks like me, a black Messiah who lives and breathes and has being in the everyday lives of black people in Britain, the United States, and Africa. It would be wrong to assume that this black Messiah is one and the same; the situations of oppression are different and so the Messiahs' features vary. Black Americans who are not necessarily at the top of their society benefit in some degree from a society that plays a part in some of the problems faced in Africa. What happens when those who are oppressed are also beneficiaries in an oppressive system? What color is Christ then? When black men oppress black women, what color is Christ? The answer is that Christ remains the core of liberative praxis, and that is rainbow colored. But this is a point that should not be forgotten: oppression is no better because it is carried out by one's own race, gender, sex, or class.

The Christ who is emerging from Africa asks far-reaching questions that can no longer be answered by development programs and well-meaning inculturating missionaries. Christ is finding authentic African voices, both male and female, and they demand to be heard on the world stage. This particular resurrection of Christ demands a radical shift of economic and cultural power rather than its legitimization in elitist hands, whether they are white or black.

3

JESUS CHRIST LIBERATOR?

The landscape for liberation in Latin America, as we saw in chapter 1, is that of dehumanizing poverty set against obscene wealth held by the few and the crushing reality of external exploitative intervention. Traditional pictures of Jesus and the salvific power of Christ had in many ways made the people ripe for victimization. If suffering unto death was what the Child of God would endure, then believing in him and gritting one's teeth under the present circumstances would ensure reward in heaven. This is too unsubtle a picture, but it is fair to say that there is a direct connection between what one believes and the social reality one is willing to endure.

The Catholic Church's arrival in Latin America heralded pain and suffering, and it preached just such a message in defense of its own exploitative policies. Like all conquerors, the church had to portray itself as the savior of otherwise oppressed and barbaric races, and it did a very good job. It is only in recent work that the biased picture painted by the recorders of pre-Christian Latin American history, who were mainly priests, has been exposed. The Christ who was preached was the One who undermined indigenous cultures and held immense social control. The Christ was the bloody Christ of conquest who laid down a social pattern that would last for centuries. People exposed to such a Christ will understand hardship and suffering as part of the Christian message. Latin Americans, along with most of Christendom, did not look for liberation in this world but were promised it in the next if they bore their suffering with Christ.

Until the 1960s the dominant theological view was that very little could be changed in the world because of the fallen nature of its inhabitants. However, a very significant theological shift took root in Latin America through the Medellín Conference of bishops. (Chapter 1 discussed this in depth.) Once attention was paid to the plight of poor people as something that could and should be overcome, the Christological discourse changed significantly. Christ was no longer simply resident in the church, which should therefore be obeyed, but was in the people, who should be raised up out of their poverty. It was no longer possible to just talk about Christ, that is, to create doctrines about Christ. Christ became part of the ongoing dialogue between oppressed and oppressors. Through this dialogue, people would end not with a definition of Christ but with an understanding of themselves and the situation in which they lived. Christ was no longer the Omega Point to be met after death but was instead the starting point for liberative praxis in the here and now. The emphasis changed from eschatology to incarnation, not that of the past but what is possible in the present. Clerics could no longer hide behind the save-all phrase that certain things are mysteries. Instead, they had to work with people to find meaning when confronted with these so-called mysteries. All these generally inspiring and potentially liberating hopes and aspirations required a new way of finding Jesus.

Jon Sobrino points out that the traditional Catholic starting point for finding Jesus has been the Council of Chalcedon with its insistence on the two natures of Jesus, the divine and the human. Such a starting point has obvious difficulties for the ordinary person[1] since the language and the concepts it conveys are not directly accessible to human intuition. If finding Jesus is a matter of intellectual athleticism, then it would be legitimate to start with and remain with such concepts as hypostatic union. However, if our quest is concerned with the reality of Jesus in our everyday lives, then such a starting point is absurd. If Rudolf Bultmann is correct in asserting that "the motivation of all theology is to be better able to comprehend our own existence,"[2] then dogmatic decrees at councils are hardly relevant.

Sobrino, as a liberation theologian, has other objections to the premises of Chalcedon, namely, that it assumes a descent Christology whereby God somehow came down and took human form. The divine and eternal burst through into human nature in a once-and-for-all way, bringing with it all the promises of eternity, indeed, personifying such things. Sobrino feels that this view overlooks the biblical idea of God being at work with the world and being involved in struggles for justice.[3] God is too abstract and Jesus too open to manipulation if we attempt to find either of them in dogma and decrees. Carter Heyward warns, "Nicea and Chalcedon's Hellenization of Jesus evolved from, and resulted in, a spiritualization of the human Jesus. The councils located his primary significance in who he was (Logos) rather than in what he did. . . . His essence relegated his actions to a place of remarkable insignificance since there is nothing remarkable about a divine man's ability to effect miraculous change."[4]

The only conclusion we can reach from such a position is that we cannot do as he did since we are not divine. It is therefore legitimate to ask whether we need to understand him since it would surely be enough to believe in him and to cite human nature as the reason we cannot emulate him. Thus, our religious quest would end in declaring Jesus as the Christ. This kind of approach should be recommended only to those who want certainty with little effort and who can bear to look at the world in which we live with no hope for its improvement. There is nothing we can do since, as Heyward says, "Relation to God gave way to an inner union of God and humanity. The Jewish tradition of voluntary activity between God and humanity collapsed in orthodox Christianity under the weight of Greek metaphysics."[5]

For those living in the oppressive environment of Latin America, such a situation is unacceptable. People who have been unable to accept this roboticized, metaphysical Jesus have attempted other approaches. They have preferred a more biblical focus to a dogmatic one. This is not necessarily a historical approach since they are trying to find the character of Jesus rather than a factual chronology. This approach makes Jesus accessible because the language is more comprehensible. However, it is not without its problems because Jesus has already been turned into theology, even in the earliest scriptures. Therefore, even at source as it were, we are presented with several Christologies, not just one. The real man is always obscured by the thoughts, hopes, and needs of others.

Many in Latin America prefer to begin where they find Jesus in worship. Sobrino puts it this way: "Once one does accept the presence of the living, resurrected Christ, then faith knows of the existence of the historical Jesus in and through the liturgical experience."[6]

Although faith does have a part to play, it is difficult to accept that Jesus can be found in this way since it is often hard to differentiate between reality and illusion. Faith can set both a conscious agenda and an unconscious agenda, which can seriously disturb the ability to discriminate. People often see what they expect to see; thus, using faith to find the historical Jesus can become a circular activity.

Sobrino argues that Christ really does not exist unless Christ offers an alternative in people's lives, but he still acknowledges that it is difficult to find what is authentic if we use this method. Christian living is more than an internal metanoia. It must be something real, something made concrete, not merely felt or pondered.[7] He is also critical of those who would envisage Jesus simply as a great model or teacher. The danger here is that Jesus becomes the model of bourgeois morality and citizenship, thus becoming a figure that can repress as much as liberate.[8] Sobrino wishes to use the historical Jesus as the starting point for understanding God and all the attendant concepts such as redemption and atonement. He believes that such a starting point avoids abstractionism. With a focus on the historical Jesus, Christ is seen in terms of knowledge and real-life praxis. Thus, people find who Christ is and how Christ saves them. Sobrino says, "Paradoxically enough it is access to the concrete Jesus that brings out his universal potentialities in diverse historical situations."[9]

Latin American liberation theology has focused on the historical Jesus for guidance and orientation. Jesus is envisaged as the midpoint between two extremes—Christ as an abstraction or Jesus of direct and immediate ideological use. Walter Kasper expresses the view that we find ourselves in an age when "it is now a matter of talking about Jesus Christ in such a way that human beings feel that they themselves and their problems are being discussed."[10]

By focusing on the historical Jesus, people do not wish to go back to first-century Palestine since that is not where contemporary problems are situated. There is also the recognition of the part we play in the problem solving, and so a very positive picture of human natures shines through. Leonardo Boff tells us, "If Jesus-man can be the incarnation of the Word, it is because there already existed this possibility within human nature."[11] He goes on to say that Christianity recognized that potential in Jesus, but in stating this, nothing strange or miraculous is being affirmed: "What is declared is the maximum realization of the human person itself in God. Thus Jesus Christ, man and God, is not a myth but the eschatological realization of the fundamental possibility that God placed in human nature."[12] The divine potential was fulfilled in Jesus, but we still have the business of our own becoming. We have the same fundamental possibility that Jesus had, and whether we develop it as fully is our own process of salvation.

What emerges in the theology of Latin America is a move from a tearful reflection on the gulf between the promises of heaven and the grim, hellish realities of earth to an examination of the causes of those realities. The standard theological answer of original sin was no longer acceptable as an inevitable and absolute answer to all the problems of suffering in the world. A new understanding of sin arose, and it was no longer viewed as a personal weakness arising from our inherited

congenital disability, original sin. Rather, it was understood as an institutional reality—one that was set in place by human hands—and
therefore, it could be dismantled by them. Nothing is inevitable about
capitalism. It is a choice made by a small percentage of the world, and
it adversely affects the rest of the world. If we take seriously God's incarnation, which even by a literalist interpretation depended on a number
of human choices, then we can have the confidence that death-induc-
ing structures can be replaced by other, more biophilic structures
through the power of human/divine choice. Sin is no more inevitable
than divine incarnation, and both are within our grasp.

The theology of Latin America seeks to reject á highly abstract
Christ and focus on Jesus in an authentic and truly operative way. This
is not by simply turning Jesus into a political animal but by viewing him
as One who loved people in a concrete and unconditional manner.
Christians are called to be open to radical love, through which the
problems of human existence can be faced and transformed. Wolfhart
Pannenberg has stated, "Theological truth is verified if it is capable of
offering a better explanation of reality."[13] It would be sufficient to
address the abstraction of sin and evil with the abstraction of Christ.
Unfortunately, sin is not abstract; it manifests itself all too clearly in
injustice and exploitation. It is encountered not in essence but in concrete circumstances. Latin American theologians view sin as alienation
and injustice, which do not just happen but which are caused. So the
Christian life can be viewed as a passover from alienation to communion, brought about by an informed engagement with the causes of
alienation and the praxis to overcome it. Christ did not merely talk
about God and human beings; Christ became a human being and in so
doing transformed humanity and history into a living temple of God.[14]
The incarnation focuses love of God in the concrete and demands that
it does not remain a self-comforting illusion. For Gustavo Gutiérrez,
the spirituality of liberation involves conversion to our neighbor[15]
because Jesus did not proclaim only God; he also proclaimed the realm
of God. Gutiérrez beautifully expresses the necessity to make concrete
the abstraction of Christ in the building of the realm:

> Christ does not spiritualise the eschatological promises, he gives
> them meaning and fulfillment today (Luke 4:21) but at the same
> time he opens new perspectives by catapulting history forward,
> forward towards total reconciliation. The hidden sense is not the
> spiritual one which devalues and even eliminates temporal and
> earthly realities as obstacles; rather it is the sense of a fullness
> which takes on and transforms historical reality. Moreover, it is

only in the temporal, earthy, historical event that we can open up to the future of complete fulfillment.[16]

This future of complete fulfillment requires us to partake of the sacrament of our neighbors, even those who have been disfigured by oppression, despoliation and alienation and who have no beauty and majesty. In solidarity with these people we make manifest the realm of God.

Sobrino also believes that Jesus, or for that matter God, cannot be understood in isolation from this realm that is fast approaching. Jesus, he claims, did not preach a message about himself or about God in isolation, and it is the relational aspect that makes the focus the coming of the realm. Sobrino wishes to untangle a knot that has been caused by the interweaving, in Christian interpretation, of God's realm and heaven. They are not by any means interchangeable concepts although they have often been used as such with negative consequences. By confusing the realm with heaven, Christian theology has given too transcendent a vista to something that Jesus understood in a more historical context. It is Sobrino's view that Jesus wished to combine transcendence and history.[17] Yet he acknowledges that it is difficult to know what the realm is because Jesus did not describe it in words; he just said it was near. He also acted as though he wished to hasten its arrival. Through examining his actions, we get a glimpse of what it is.

Sobrino is in line with other liberation theologians by declaring that the realm is liberative as witnessed by Jesus' actions toward poor, oppressed, and sick people. However, he points out that the approach of the realm is not universal but only partial and scandalous.[18] It is addressed to the concerns of those usually considered beneath contempt. They will enter this realm when justice is served. Indeed, Jesus practiced the realm predominantly with outcasts. The reason, then, why it was scandalous is self-evident while it was partial, both in its proclamation and in the fact that the cause of justice was never, and has never been, served as it should with persons on the margins of society. Jesus imaged the realm as an all-inclusive meal, a great banquet of joy and fulfillment. It is no wonder that Christians, if they are realistic, have to acknowledge the partial nature of this event. While people starve and toil under oppressive regimes, it is un-Christian to declare that the realm is here. Such a declaration only highlights our lack of faith that the insights of Christ may be made manifest.

Latin American theology is nevertheless positive about human nature, believing it capable of bringing the realm into concrete existence. The metaphysical realities of God and heaven are not denied, but the emphasis is on the expression of both through orthopraxis. Carlos Mesters argues that if evil exists, you should examine your conscience since "you have closed your heart and have not helped others to grow. The misery of this world is neither an excuse nor a motive for flight, but an accusation against yourself. It is not you who should judge misery, but misery judges you and your system and makes you see its defects (Matthew 7:1–5)."[19]

The picture that emerges of Christ is of One who has gone before us and understands the pitfalls but is no longer willing to excuse the Divine Self or us on the grounds of metaphysical congenital disabilities. After all, Jesus had no knowledge of doctrines of original sin. His heritage spoke of people working with God to set in place historical change. The realm of God was not viewed as a divine gift simply to be graciously received by awestruck bystanders; it was and is a divine imperative that involves the whole of creation in a passionate struggle for justice. The inability to struggle in this way is not because of the devil or fallen nature. It is because of lack of passion. Unfortunately, the churches have set the scene for Christians to be cautious and lacking in passion. Fire in the belly has been viewed with suspicion for centuries, and once passion is coupled with an understanding that hell awaits the one who gets it wrong, it is not surprising that moral paralysis has developed in the Christian world. The emphasis on orthodoxy rather than passionate action has for centuries inhibited creative engagement with the world.

This is understandable if the reason for the incarnation is seen as payment of a debt to God and the incarnate life as a standard by which all will be found wanting in the end. However, if Christ is the culmination of history and One who allows others to follow, Christians can become much more adventurous in their relationships with one another and the created order. Boff, while being positive about human nature, does not really encourage the idea of imagination:

> He [Jesus] is the One who first arrived at the terminus of the journey to give us hope and certainty that we too are destined to be what He has become; if we live what He lived, we too will have a similar end. Christ's perfection is not historical chance nor merely an anthropological success. For all eternity, He was predestined by God to become the human who could realize all the capacities of being one with God.[20]

Christ became incarnate not because of sin, but because human nature desires to reach its own divination. The person Jesus of

Nazareth was born as a result of a long process of cosmic evolution. This process did not end with his birth but continued throughout his life as he grew to perfection. However, Boff declares that the true cosmic dimension of Christ is revealed in the resurrection: "Resurrection is therefore the eschatologization of a human being who has arrived at the end of the evolutionary process and been inserted into the divine reality."[21]

By it Christ did not leave the world but penetrated it more profoundly and therefore is present in all reality (Matt. 28:20). Christ opened up a new dimension in human and divine fullness. That this event should be witnessed in earthly conditions underlines the meaning of the incarnation, which is that there is no separation between divine and human once the human has been expanded to its limits. Boff believes that through the resurrection, Christ is glorified and present in each being.[22]

However, even Boff, who suggests something quite radical, stops short of our complete freedom to engage experimentally with the world around us. He wants us to follow the exact path of Jesus. In many ways this re-creates the problems it has solved because we are back to asking very specific questions about the historical reality of Jesus that are either impossible to answer or not that informative in our present age if we do answer them. There are also difficulties with the notion of predestination because it precludes choice, which is foundational in liberation theology. Even if we understand this notion of predestination as an evolutionary event—that the divine and human natures are so alike that eventually the divine will burst forth in the human—we need to face a problem. Scientific evolution does not understand the end product to be already decided; there is not some perfect example of the species toward which the not-yet-perfect are advancing. Religious/spiritual evolution, on the other hand, does hold this view. (We will see that this is not necessarily the case in feminist theology where the outcome is often viewed as far more open ended.) What seems to have happened is that liberation theologians are still working within given frameworks but moving the edges. Over this crucial question of the purposes of Jesus, they slide back toward orthodoxy, which results in an answer that is a cross between Platonic Ideal Forms and Darwinian evolution, when in truth they cannot have it both ways.

Latin American theology is left with the difficulty of Jesus' death if it is no longer to be understood in traditional terms as for the forgiveness of sins. Sobrino argues that the traditional view glorifies suffering and by implication encourages us to see our personal suffering as a sign of our salvation.[23] It also gives us a very questionable view of love, a view that could make us victims in the name of compassion and loving connection. Sobrino does not deny that the Scriptures speak about the death of Jesus being positive for humankind;[24] however, the elaboration of that into Jesus dying to expiate sin or as a seal of a new covenant with his blood is not the way we should view it.[25] Sobrino believes that the cross challenges us to discover what sort of God we believe in, but he is reluctant to conclude that it is a vengeful God who requires sacrifice. The traditional view can give us the idea that Jesus died once and for all and what we now need to do is to claim our own individual salvation as a result of it. This is easily criticized because it encourages too personal and inactive a view of salvation.

There is a positive view amid these apparent negatives: that God is willing and able to suffer verifies the Christian claim that God is love,[26] to love even unto death, thereby not running away from principles declared to have eternal relevance. A way to recover the original meaning of the cross is to see it as a consequence of Jesus' life, not as the total meaning of his life. We may see the cross as "the outcome of an incarnation situated in a world of sin that is revealed to be a power working against the God of Jesus."[27] Jesus' very existence was seen as an accusation against those in power who manipulated their deity to increase their own importance and position in the world. Jesus had to choose whether to wield oppressive power in the name of God or whether to pursue the loving and liberating God (Matt. 4:1–11). In this way, "the path to the cross is nothing else but a questioning search for the true God and for the true essence of power. Is power meant to oppress people or to liberate them?"[28]

Jesus proclaimed good news, which was freedom through love and truth. This stood in complete contradiction to a God who wanted to subjugate human beings through a coercive use of power. As Ernst Käsemann points out, "Any Creator who can set in opposition to his creation is a false God and false gods can turn even the pious into inhuman people."[29]

Sobrino thinks it is saying too little about Jesus to say he died because of some design of God. He thinks it is more appropriate to say he died because he would not evade his responsibility for proclaiming the liberating God in a world that lusted after power. It was not his sacrifice that was required in order to bring salvation but his commitment to liberating action, which sets the example for continuing salvation. This understanding transforms the spiritual significance of the cross. It is no longer a sign of sadness, pain, and sorrow passively accepted. Rather, it becomes a regrettable price we too may have to pay if we stand against false power and false gods. In this way Christian spirituality is not one that revels in suffering but one that values resolve and the pursuit of the true, loving God.[30] This view should make Christians a great deal more cautious about suffering than they have hitherto been. If suffering is seen as salvific, then embracing it at every turn with Christ is to be praised. Indeed, we have a Christian history littered with the scarred and broken bodies of those who have held this view. However, suffering does not bring salvation and so should be avoided where possible. What is witnessed in the life of Jesus, and required by his followers, is action that is just. In a world filled with injustice this is viewed as a countercultural position and may carry a price.

Christians should attempt to avoid and alleviate suffering wherever possible. Yet we may not become comfortable, for as Leonardo Boff says, Christ is the great element of discomfort in the world who challenges us because "he does not allow himself to be domesticated by a theological system."[31] The Christ of liberation theology expects us to be the same discomfort on the world. Therefore, if we follow Christ, we too may find ourselves on the receiving end of the big stick of ecclesiastical or political power. Our strength to endure should come from commitment and passion, not from ideas of salvific martyrdom.

The development of process thought and liberation theology has, in my opinion, brought us to a more positive place of rest. Human nature is not innately bad, and God is not inherently vengeful and judgmental. Latin American thought shows us that our own becoming is not meaningful, or really possible, in isolation. Salvation is a joint effort involving standing up for justice in society, which we could call the building of the realm on earth. It is a very powerful message. In recent years it has been acknowledged that its principles have not always been applied to women. Certainly in theory, the guilt of Eve has been lifted from our shoulders, but in practice, very little has changed and the position of women has to be seen as a priority in the struggle for social justice.

Rosemary Ruether notes with some regret that there is a very ambivalent relationship between classical liberation theology and the blossoming women's movement.[32] Among the fathers of liberation theology, Gutiérrez is one who stands proud. But there is no lead to be found from him on these matters. He insists that feminist theology is alien to the Latin American reality and is a diversion from "the primary concern of liberation theology for the poor."[33] Despite the blatant reality that feminist theology has grown in Peru over the last twenty years and therefore must be speaking to somebody, Gutiérrez holds his line and will not have it taught at his institute.

Gutiérrez also overlooks ecumenism, ecology, and indigenous spirituality, seeing them as less important than the struggle against poverty.

It is particularly surprising that he will not acknowledge the place of indigenous spirituality since his background is indigenous and not Spanish. It is also frightening that he cannot see the relationship between the broad spectrum of issues that he chooses to ignore and poverty, which he wishes to address.

Peru has a large number of right-wing, Opus Dei bishops, which no doubt makes Gutiérrez feel somewhat exposed. He has, it seems, decided to find himself a space that can be defended against the onslaught of the right-wing church. To do this he has not been daring enough to include the issues that are like red flags to the Curia. This highlights how careful we have to be in uncritically accepting that liberation theology is always a revolutionary and transforming step. It too can have its limitations. Gutiérrez illustrates how difficult it is to pursue the cause of justice on all fronts. In this way he is making his own point that preference has to be brought into play. He is no longer part of the class he prioritizes, the poor. It also has to be noted that in limiting liberation dialogue to the poor, he limits the potential of the movement. Gutiérrez is to be applauded for his foundational work and not to be totally condemned for his compromise with a right-wing church. Perhaps he has not yet thought of ways to subvert its power over him and is not ready to be crucified.

PRESENTE—LATINA WOMEN

Despite lack of support from their male colleagues, women in Latin America have been forging ahead with their own praxis for twenty years or so. Some of the impetus to do so came from feminist movements that had been established in Latin America since the beginning of the century. However, Catholic theologians in Latin America showed as much concern over connections with secular movements as feminist theologians in other parts of the world. The secular agendas were feared, and in Catholic countries the secular focus on sexual and reproductive rights was viewed as far too radical a place to start. Connection and commitment to EATWOT have probably been a greater spur to the women's theology movement and have been on hand as the movement gathered momentum over time.

It would not be fair to say that this is where the theological movements started. In true liberation style they started with the needs of the people for the basics in life. With reductions in access to food, health, and education, grassroots groups, consisting of a range of individuals with diverse backgrounds, got together to provide what they could. Reflection started in those groups and spread from there, in part, to the institutions. Catholic women have traditionally had restricted access to theological education, so the limited nature of the access for feminist theology is not at all surprising. Some of the Protestant seminaries are developing women's studies programs, but probably the greatest amount of reflection is generated from the grassroots organizations such as Talitha Cumi in Peru and Con-spirando in Santiago.

Not atypically, if the women were included at all by the male theologians, they were not considered to have anything of real importance to say. Theirs was to be the female face of otherwise unaltered doctrine. Also not atypically, women did not find this a satisfactory inclusion and began to find for themselves many eye-opening things in the Bible. As the maternal face of God was uncovered in Scripture, women felt confident to assert their place in the company of the faithful. It was similar to the early movements in European secular feminism that have now acquired the name of liberal. They were more concerned with finding a place for women within the existing systems than they were with challenging the fabric of the systems. However, just as their secular sisters had found, this kind of inclusion is not very satisfactory. For the most part it depends on the goodwill of the men in the institutions, and it can never really overcome the glass ceiling, a phenomenon that is so transparent that it is hard to prove.

This realization led women to desire the ability to name themselves, that is, to be able to forward the cause of their own liberation through their own means. The desire placed them in a critical position in relation to the church and in relation to Western feminist theology, which they claimed did not hear their voice or call them by name. The desire to name themselves placed Hispanic women at risk. They had to find a name and were not sure that one existed. As Latin American women moved through the latter part of the 1980s and into the 1990s, they realized that the risk was all they had. Classical liberation theology appeared not to have worked that well, economic situations were as bad as ever— and worse in some places—and women's voices were still perceived as distant echoes in relation to male agendas. They had to take the risk; they had to find a voice. Apart from stating how they wished to be treated in society, they had to critically examine biblical texts and reject those that justified their silence and inferior position. The authority to do this was thought to lie in Jesus Christ the liberator. The same Christ that the male theologians were talking about acted as the impetus for women to declare their own glorious and saved humanity and in so doing to reject much that the Scriptures and the churches said about them. They even had to reflect upon the nature of Christ and ask if Christ was, in fact, their liberator. Much is paradoxical in movements for liberation.

Raquel Rodriguez,[34] for example, reflects on the nature of Jesus that emerges from the story of the Samaritan woman at the well. Jesus enables women to open their eyes to possibilities that they could never in their wildest dreams imagine. The woman in the story is not blind but cannot see beyond the water in the jar, which according to Rodriguez symbolizes her own tradition. Jesus tells her that the water is no good. She will never quench her thirst from it and will have to keep coming back for more and going away at best temporarily satisfied. He urges her to break with it all and leave the water jug behind, to see beyond the limits of its edge. She must do this because he is the One who would come, not the One contained in the jar.

There is a hint of process thought here and the idea that Christ is an ever-unfolding event who cannot be contained. Indeed, those who do contain Christ are not surveying the whole picture; they are drinking in such a way that their thirst remains. Their image of Jesus Christ cannot be of the liberator since the same snares and traps keep reappearing. They are unquenched by the myopic traditions that have arisen. Christ becomes the refillable water jar and not the living water. The story of the Samaritan woman encourages Latin American women to look beyond the militarism, violence, external debt, and ecological disaster surrounding them. There are within the wider scheme answers to these questions once they have freedom from the rim of the jar. Many have understood this as meaning that the hierarchical manner in which both church and state operate only reinvents the problems they claim to solve. Christ the conqueror or even Christ the liberator leaves women thirsty.

Christ the liberator, when conveyed through male hands, has not always realized that the God of the poor is in truth the God of women. This is the case because women are among the very poorest in Latin America. Liberation theologians have, for the most part, failed to comprehend the significant difference that this makes when considering ways to empower poor people.

Presente: **My Body**

Another, but related, area left almost untouched by the male Christ of liberation is that of reproductive rights. No connection was made between poverty and reproductive rights. There is also a striking silence on domestic violence and backstreet abortions, which is perhaps a good thing since most liberation theologians take a decidedly Vatican line when dealing with these issues. It has to be acknowledged that not many women are vocal on these matters either. Ivone Gebara is one of the few to speak in favor of legalizing abortion. Her view is based on the realization that women will always have to resort to abortion. There are between 36 and 53 million abortions a year worldwide, of which 30 to 50 percent are illegal. Gebara is realistic and would rather that women had safe choices.[35]

The issue of reproductive rights in Latin America is not as straightforward as in Europe because of what has been called contraceptive imperialism. There has historically been interference in governmental population policies by multinational companies and development agencies. This has ranged from applying pressure for widespread sterilization to flooding the countries with hormonal contraceptives that have not been properly tested. While feminists are keen to resist this kind of intervention, they are also keen to give women control over their own bodies.

Victory of a kind was won at the Cairo International Conference on Population and Development in 1994. At that conference the Vatican made its famous and staggering alliance with Muslim fundamentalists in order to prevent the inclusion of reproductive rights and abortion in the final conference document. Women's organizations from north and south were successful in preventing this unholy alliance from achieving its aims. It was perhaps a first, but significant, move toward women being placed at the center of debates about reproductive rights and abortion.

It would be too easy to say that the reason such questions have not been addressed by the liberating Christ is the machismo in Latin American countries. This is in part true because it makes women invisible. However, a celibate male clergy, modeling the life of Christ, add to the silence because they do not see the problem. The Christ of liberation has not been released quite enough from the straitjacket of dualistic metaphysics despite Christ's new, historic look. This focus on a Christ who is in some way complete, whole, and celibate relegates all questions involving sexual ethics to the margins.

Feminist theologians, on the other hand, are not afraid to deal with the fleshy reality of Jesus and connect it with their own lives. Maria Clara Bingemer[36] argues that women's bodies are eucharistic. She understands the eucharist to refer to the incarnation, death, and resurrection of Jesus Christ and declares that women "possess in their bodiliness the physical possibility of performing the divine eucharistic action. In the whole process of gestation, childbirth, protection and nourishing of a new life, the sacrament of the eucharist, the divine act, happens anew."[37]

What exactly is she saying? Are women the Christ of the eucharist? What difference, if any, does she see between the divine action of the eucharist and the divine creative action of women? It appears there is no difference. She extends the divinely creative actions of women's bodies beyond those of giving birth to toiling in the fields and factories in order to provide life for others. Most of all the bodies of women in Latin America are placed in the struggle for liberation. She says, "Woman's body, eucharistically given to the struggle for liberation, is really and physically distributed, eaten and drunk by those who will— as men and women of tomorrow—continue the same struggle."[38]

We almost hear the words "take, eat, this is my body" as we picture women standing against the many faces of oppression afflicting them. Bingemer moves the Christological debate on many steps when she equates the bodies of women with the eucharistic body of Christ—not least because these are real bodies that experience the pleasures and pains of being fully incarnate. These women laugh, cry, love, hate, make love, are raped or beaten, are violated by the system, and often abuse others. Can these bodies really be the body of Christ in the eucharistic sense? A resounding yes is the answer. Bingemer is referring to women as the body of Christ not in the community sense of church but in their own embodied existence, in both the good and the bad. Their embodied struggle is the essence of Christ. This places a new slant on Jesus as *compañero*, or fellow revolutionary. He has been understood almost as the ultimate revolutionary. This is not, however, the way in which some feminists wish to see him. His part in their struggle is far more intimate. He is not their leader: he is the struggle; he is their embodiment within it.

An Indecent Christ

In this way Jesus becomes an indecent Christ. Marcella Althaus-Reed proposes an indecent theology, which she develops from her background in Argentina where women were defined through the concept of decency. It was a concept that entered Latin America with the conquistadors: "It is closely related to the objectification of women as property through the institution of colonial marriage, the exaltation of reproduction amongst the white, foreign elite under judicial superstructure committed to inheritance laws, and also to the confinement of women in certain legal [although the word used is 'decent'] physical, emotional and economic spaces."[39]

Women on the margins of this tightly regulated society rebelled against decency either through choice or through necessity. The categories did not fit their lived experience. They were unable to be defined and contained by imperial inventions, and in their indecency they found new, life-giving ways. Women who worked in factories or took part in revolutionary struggle were defined as indecent and were seen as sexually available. Through the embodiment of these women, Christ is indecent, the One who expands the edges of categories and seeks life.

The Christ who is bursting out in Latin America is not simply the classical liberation Christ of the poor. Women have brought new dimensions such as color, race, and ecology. The observation of the five hundred years of resistance in 1992 (the alternative to the glorification of Columbus) highlighted awareness of color oppression and exposed Christian attitudes to indigenous spirituality. Elsa Tamez from Costa Rica has focused on the need to understand indigenous spirituality rather than adopt a superior position as Christianity has done since its imposition in Latin America.[40] She is working toward a theology of liberation that takes liberating aspects from both traditions while condemning the parts of both traditions that have been perverted and led to moral enslavement. She is aware that women have to be particularly alert during this process since both traditions have not treated them with the dignity and equity they deserve. Tamez is looking for the Christ who can critique and be critiqued by the traditions that came before Christ's conquering soldiers. This is quite a radical move—one that feminists worldwide should heed. There is still an unforgivable tendency by some to see Jesus as the One who put all the previous wrongs right and saved women from stifling cultures. What Tamez is attempting in Latin America could be profitable in Europe among Jewish, Muslim, Hindu, and Christian feminists.

Nelly Ritchie from Argentina would be in sympathy with Tamez's adventure since her Christ has "nothing to do with an applied doctrine but with a truth to discover, with a response which, translated into words and deeds, takes on historical truthfulness and liberating force."[41] This Christ as known on a "continent that is bleeding to death" has no interest in private salvation but moves toward the liberation of the whole people. Therefore, the white invaders cannot find solace in a belief that they will be saved while the continent perishes. The task of liberation involves all the people who inhabit the continent. "Christian" is not a defining term but a cosmic vision, and Christ can no longer be used to disguise reality or to exclude people. Latin American women are dialoguing with Christ from their own reality in search of lines of action that are liberating. For example, the Mothers of the Plaza del Mayo, who weep and witness to their missing children, embody liberative praxis in their struggle against powerlessness. They are a resurrection people in that they refuse the final triumph of death, which in this case would be silence. They are in a real sense witnessing to a new life simply by being there; the disappearances and probable deaths of their children have given life to their own struggle and resistance. They witness to hope in the face of fear and despair.

Ritchie argues that we find a powerful example of our capacities by looking to the woman who anointed Jesus. Here was a woman who was condemned and marginalized, yet "she was for Jesus—the Christ—someone who was not afraid to let others know how she felt, who loved unconditionally, who offered what she had, and who anointed him with her life."[42] She loved fully and in so doing revealed the Christ to Jesus. Latin America has many such Christs, women who keep going, women who scratch out livings in order to feed their children, women who perhaps sell their bodies in order to get food for their children. These women are no longer to be judged but to be seen as Christ for their loved ones and for us, the more privileged, who can see the fullness of their love. This is not to romanticize the situation or to justify the existence of such dire circumstances. Liberation still requires that they should not have to pay so dearly to love so fully. However, what is graphically illustrated is that Christ is love in its fullness in the midst of the struggle, whatever means are used to carry on.

Christ the Web of Liberation

The Mexican theologian María Pilar Aquino is clear that the means necessary for the struggle to be successful is a thorough understanding of the way in which gender oppression operates. This involves a critical analysis of race, class, and culture as well as economics. Latin American women have to fully understand how their position in society developed in order to systematically resist and change it. Simply engaging with theology will not actually change society. The resistance has to be from many angles, and women have to find their own language in all areas of resistance.

Aquino images Jesus as the One who wished liberation for all, and since it is clearly not visible in the lives of women, he would encourage the continuation of the redemptive process by those who follow him. She is aware that women will have to do this for themselves because male theologians have not even come close to addressing the problems of women. She also encourages a closer working relationship with secular feminists since they have already started the work of social analysis that is crucial to the next resistance in feminist theology. She calls for more connection with indigenous spirituality and a conscious connection over class and race lines. For Aquino the great lie that the followers of Jesus have to expose—and quickly—is that the current economic system is not the democratizing force that it claims to be. The truth is that it enslaves and dehumanizes a large percentage of the world's population. Aquino wants the dehumanized to find a common voice and expose the grand lie.[43] It is curious that against this background Christ who has been used to underpin universal claims and absolutist traditions takes on a role reversal. The Christ who exposes the grand, universal lie of advanced capitalism cannot be One who looks for universals and absolute power bases. Christ both critiques and is critiqued by the mass destruction that springs from thinking in universal absolutes.

Ivone Gebara is among those who acknowledge that the time of striving for absolute and universally applicable truth is over. She believes that we all have to name our context, and in so doing we then allow connections to be made between us that are far more real than those imposed from outside. She believes that certain themes will emerge from most contexts because these things unite us as human beings. This belief can be criticized on the grounds that it sounds suspiciously like natural moral law, which the Catholic Church has used over the centuries to its own ends. However, the things that Gebara would see as emerging are quite distinct from those of the fathers of the church. Her focus is on a desire to feed our children and to live in peace.

Gebara thinks that Christian theology has to be conducted from the broadest ecumenical base. Christ must not exclude or be seen in such a way as to allow those who define Christ to exert power over others. She has found that by understanding Christ as part of the Trinity, her way forward has been easier. Christ can be seen as part of a basic matrix of life that illustrates the creative power of interconnection,[44] a matrix that exists because of diversity and thrives on it. In this way Christ is also understood as part of the matrix of creation and the diversity inherent in it. By illustrating her understanding of Christ in this, Gebara highlights that each individual is in a web of relations that include other people and the earth itself. The trinitarian Christ is within this strong, yet fragile, web of life.

Gebara's approach is refreshing. It opens up the possibility of growth and diversity. We can say that the web's strength is preserved when all accept diversity and allow it to blossom. However, the fragility becomes immediately apparent when the will to power is exerted. This damages and may even break the web, and all are made vulnerable, although it may take the aggressors a little longer than everyone else to realize it. Christ as imaged by Gebara can never be used as a stick with which to beat others because this is contrary to the interrelated nature of Christ's own existence. Christ as part of the web of life casts a very different face of God on the earth. We have to dispense with the all-powerful, ruling, and controlling image, which disrupts the web. God loses unilateral power, and we are made to accept the reality that all is in process. Therefore, we cannot simply project a future paradise. We have to work for it now and live with the fear and failure as much as the joy and success.

It is inspiring to see how even when Jesus Christ is declared liberator, there is always more to the liberation than meets the eye. Male liberation theologians truly believed that they had found the Christ who would free all. Jesus Christ was no longer the One who declared hidden truths to which only the initiated could have access. Jesus Christ was the One who made us fight against oppression that all could see. However, female oppression was not evident to the eyes of the male clergy who formed the cutting edge of the liberation movement. In pointing this out I do not wish to suggest that the women have seen the whole picture or spoken the final word; rather, they have found new vistas of liberation that require attention. The mistake of the men was to suppose that they had found the answer because their approach suggested that some answers could be found for the marginalized. In assuming that this was the answer they have made the same mistake that religion has always made. This is regrettable but not exactly unpredictable. After all, totally new models are hard to imagine and develop, so old habits can easily be accommodated despite one's best resolutions.

Jesus' struggle was against any force that dehumanized the people around him. Therefore, it is rather naive of Gutiérrez to claim that the feminist struggle is not one for Latin American women or that ecological issues are secondary to those affecting poor people. Violation of nature and women devalues both and should be fought against. It could be said that anytime the liberation struggle appears too narrow, it may not be liberation at all. While it has to be acknowledged that we personally cannot fight all the battles, we can and should align ourselves with those who struggle on other fronts, in this way expanding the web of which Gebara speaks.

The Christ of liberation points to the depth of human experience as the place in which we find the Divine. Freeing human beings into fuller experiences of what it is to be alive and without chains is a task of divine importance. It is a task that can be fully undertaken only by real engagement with people. As Joan Casanas puts it, "My God is the people, comrade; alluring and demanding."[45]

This demanding God does not know the answers but is alive in the questions. Latin American liberation theology alerts us to the difficulties in assuming that even the most radical answer is the answer. The world may now be a smaller place, increasingly dominated by global economics, but it is a place that requires a greater spectrum of approaches if liberation is to succeed. A new insight that women have brought to the debate is the realization that liberation is not a once-and-for-all achievement. It is not so much a final destination as a journey with a variety of stations along the way. Some we may wish to return to; others we would be happy to erase from the map. Christ, then, is not some kind of Omega Point or Cosmic/Divine Navigator; Christ is a fellow pilgrim, a revolutionary, or a victim, always deeply embedded in the reality of the situation, not hovering above in a Disney World of happy endings.

4

REDEEMER OR REDEEMED?

With the rise of feminist consciousness in the late fifties in the United States, Christian women began to examine their situation in the churches and as represented in dominant theology. The secular movement was telling women to value their own experience while theology still held many negative statements and assumptions about the nature of women. Despite the attempts of Elizabeth Cady Stanton in the nineteenth century, very little had changed in traditional theology regarding the role of women. With the production of the Woman's Bible Stanton had highlighted the sexist nature of much Christian Scripture. The project, which exposed a self-evident truth—that the Bible contains a great deal of literature that either ignores women or treats them as chattel—had little impact on the establishment. Stanton's optimism and hard work went largely unfulfilled, and any gains were undone or absorbed into the status quo. Like its secular sister, Christian feminism all but died out in the next generation.

It would be hard to argue that the second wave of feminism in the late fifties was fueled by its nineteenth-century foresisters. Most of the momentum came from the civil rights movement. Women who had been in the forefront of that movement found that while civil rights were being granted in society, their requests for rights within the churches were being ridiculed and largely ignored. Christian women were hearing of the value of their own experience from the secular movement while being silenced within their own tradition. Rosemary Ruether points out, "Religious traditions fall into crisis when the received interpretation of the redemptive paradigms contradict experience in significant ways."[1]

No doubt the women of the twentieth century experienced the same frustrations and feelings of denial that their nineteenth-century sisters had felt, but their situation was rather different. Two significant theological advances helped women value their own experience, liberation theology and process thought. It would be a mistake to say that either movement paid the attention to women that it might have done. Nonetheless, the tools became available for women to convert their experience into a sustained theological challenge. The question that feminist theologians felt able to address in a new, positive, and exciting way was, Who is God for women, and how does Jesus redeem us? They felt that it was no longer necessary to settle for the depressing answer that God is our Judge and Jesus our Savior since he atoned for the sin brought to the world by woman. The male concept of God consistently denied women access to institutions and often, it seemed, to full humanity. If God is constantly imaged as male, there is little room for women to play a part in the divine drama, except a negative one.

Mary Daly, in characteristic fashion, declared that we have to do away with the word "God" because it conjures up Yahweh, the old patriarch and warrior king. She called for a radical new naming, a moving forward from empty symbols and oppressive structures to a search for new, transforming images.[2] This renaming of God is not merely a cosmetic operation; Daly sees it as extremely important for the becoming of women. In *Beyond God the Father*, she says, "The divine patriarch castrates women as long as he is allowed to live on in the human imagination. The process of cutting away the supreme phallus can hardly be a merely rational affair. The problem is one of transforming the collective imagination so that this distortion of the human aspiration to transcendence loses its credibility."[3]

Process thought enables us to see beyond God the Father, since God's becoming is tied up with us. If we are female, then God becomes as we become, in female form and experience. Daly sees this as bound up with language and ways of imaging God: "As a uniquely masculine image and language for divinity loses credibility so also the idea of a single divine incarnation in a human being of the male sex may give way in the religious consciousness to an increased awareness of the power of Being in all persons."[4]

Daly does not deny that a revelatory event took place in the person of Jesus. Rather, she affirms that it can be revealed at every historical moment in every culture and individual life. Daly declares that the male God carries too many bad memories and images for women. Further, to use a word generally considered to be male about one's own process as a female seems perverse. I have sympathy with the theologians who ask whether a male Savior and a male God can save women.

Mary Daly believes we must move to a post-Christian era, while Rosemary Radford Ruether and Elisabeth Schüssler Fiorenza believe women can find redemption through Christ. For Schüssler Fiorenza, "feminist spirituality has to grow out of a feminist theology as a critical theology of liberation. The task of such a theology is to uncover Christian theological traditions and myths that perpetuate sexist ideologies violence and alienation. . . . The Church has publicly to confess that it has wronged women."[5]

Before it will do that, it will have to be shown the negative aspects that emanate from a wholly male view of God. Churches are naive to assume that a male symbol for God has no far-reaching effects. Any symbol carries with it certain assumptions that affect society, not just the deity itself. Religious symbols are supposed to speak authentically to all, but this has not been the case with the male deity. It has to be examined in the light of the experience of those who have been excluded.

Women who reflected on the denial of their personhood within the churches began to realize that the way God and Christ were imaged had a major part to play in their exclusion. They also realized that whatever diminished their full humanity was not redemptive. Further, they were not mere echoes of men, and their experiences were unique and valid but absent in Christian theology. Mary Daly clearly states the case: "If God in 'His' heaven is a father ruling 'His' people, then it is in the nature of things and according to divine plan and the order of the universe that society be male dominated."[6]

She goes on to suggest that the assumption of order and ruling leads to definite patterns in society. A mystification of roles takes place whereby, for example, the husband dominating his wife is seen to represent God himself. In this way the Judeo-Christian tradition has legitimized a sexually imbalanced society in which women are oppressed. Daly asserts that there is nothing innately divine in this scheme. It is the images and values of a given society being projected into the realm of belief. Once they are there they seem to have an unchangeable, independent existence and validity of their own. God who was to be women's hope becomes a divine patriarch and "the Jesus who was to be their brother has the face of their colonial master,"[7] and society is divided into us and them. The roles and stereotypes of patriarchy have been developed and sustained by creating an artificial polarization of human qualities in traditional sexual stereotypes. If God is seen as male, then men can project the qualities they value and not vice versa. The eternal masculine stereotype tends to imply rationality, objectivity, aggression, the ability to dominate and manipulate people and the environment, and the tendency to construct boundaries between the self and others. If this stereotype is to exist, it has to create an opposite caricature, which is exactly opposite of the male stereotype—emotional, passive, sensuous. This latter quality has caused problems for women in Christianity. The *Malleus Maleficarum* of the fifteenth century says women are most involved with witchcraft since "all witchcraft comes from carnal lust, which is in women insatiable."[8] Millions of women paid with their lives.

Men are saved from this because of their rationality and the fact that Jesus was a man. What else could he be, since God would not enter inferior female flesh? If women object to their stereotype, Christianity can reinforce it by quoting the male God figure and the suffering, meek, self-abasing Savior. Women have been conditioned to see any act that affirms the worth of the female ego as blameworthy. The male God has gone deep, so deep that women have learned to distrust themselves. Anybody who does not reflect the image of the male God/Christ is an outsider, whether nonwhite, nonheterosexual, or a woman.

As women strove for wholeness through the civil rights and women's movements, such a neurotic, vindictive God lost his appeal. If God is to remain relevant to feminists, then the image has to move from oppression to self-actualization and social commitment. As feminism declares women's human dignity and gives them increased opportunities to express it in society, a great spiritual moment is awakened. We get the chance to express our own divinity and to enable and empower society as a result of this action. The becoming of women also challenges the old moral order because many of the Christian virtues have been based on male understanding of what it is to be godly. A major part of such a system is seeing sin as offending against those in power who are often viewed as representing God. In this scheme, oppression is not a sin; it may even be a virtue if it keeps people God-fearing. Theology has created an unholy morality that no longer serves life because of its insistence in focusing on only half the story, that is, male experience and proclamations about the Divine.

Male Christ, Liberated Female?

Ruether finds the origin of this denial of the feminine in the classical Neoplatonism and apocalyptic Judaism out of which Christianity was born. Here we find the combination of a male warrior God with the exaltation of the intellect over the body. The alienation of the masculine from the feminine is the basic sexual symbol that sums up all the other dualisms, which are mind and body; subjective self and objective world; individual and community; autonomous will (male) and bodily sensuality (female) and the domination of nature by spirit.[9]

Under such a system, it is probably impossible to work out the basic conviction that human beings are in the image of God. According to Ruether, the dualism of patriarchal religion is not the only aspect that discourages us from claiming our own divinity. She says the parent model of the Divine confronts us with a neurotic God who does not want us to grow up.[10] To become autonomous and responsible is a great sin while spiritual infancy is a virtue. Ruether points out that there was a time when God was far more encouraging. The business of reminding us of our divinity included putting down the mighty, releasing captives, and vindicating the oppressed. She says, "If he could be it again he would free slaves, include Gentiles and perhaps even women."[11]

Ruether is quite confident that it can happen again because with the death of Jesus, the Heavenly Ruler has left the heavens and been poured out on the earth: "A new God is being born in our hearts to teach us to level the heavens and exalt the earth and create a new world without masters and slaves, rulers and subjects."[12]

There can be no claiming of divinity for anyone while injustice and inequality stalk the earth. Ruether is keen to unleash the human potential bound by patriarchy because a tradition that promised a prophetic liberating tradition cannot be left in the hands of its per-verters and made into a static set of ideas. Ruether points out that language has been manipulated by the Christian tradition, for exam-ple, servanthood language when used by Jesus meant that we are free from obligations to human hierarchies of power. Yet when imperial Christianity used the same language, it reinforced the servitude of sub-jugated people.[13] Jesus rejected the notion that religion could sanctify dominant hierarchies (Matt. 20:26–28), yet strangely the church has kept hierarchies. The church has been able to do this by blunting the social edge of the gospel and spiritualizing Jesus' message.

Feminist theology is not asserting unprecedented ideas when it defines the prophetic, liberating tradition as the norm. Indeed, women are manifesting God's liberating action by declaring the least first and the first last. In so doing feminist theologians are turning Christian doctrine on its head. They are questioning the naturally subordinate place of women stemming from Eve. The subordination of women holds in place many of the pivotal Christian doctrines such as the Fall, original sin, atonement, and redemption. By rejecting this guilt trap, women are opening up the theological landscape. However, many still think that any attempt to change this order and give women equality is rebellion against the divine will.

CHRIST THE REDEEMER

Throughout Christian history, there has been what Schüssler Fiorenza calls "the egalitarian counter-cultural trend," which has spoken about the equality of women. This trend has usually been connected with ascetic sects, which have been condemned as heretical. Yet there have been snatches of this trend in movements that, though not dominant, escaped condemnation. For example, it comes through in Protestantism in left-wing utopian and mystical sects such as the German Rappists or Anglo-American Shakers who felt a male Christ was totally inadequate because he could not reveal the female nature of God. Mysticism with its direct relation to God has enabled women to have authority and autonomy against patriarchs. The same is true of some religious houses that have valued the gifts of women. However, it was often the case that the dominant tradition and God the Father, Ruler, and Judge in time regained his power. Women who resisted the loss of their privileges were often sent to the stake as vehicles of the devil.

For some kinds of deviant Christianity, equality in Christ actually meant a new relationship between men and women within the churches. Montanism and Gnosticism did not scapegoat women but gave them equal prophetic authority and participation in ordinary ministry. Dominant Christianity would defend itself by saying that it never denied equality in Christ, but this was in a spiritualized way. The actual nuts and bolts of everyday equality were hardly given a thought. Although Gnosticism argued it was necessary to transcend our sexual bodily nature, it felt women could do this as effectively as men. It is sad and ironic that the church, which should be the haven of women's dignity and full humanity, declared heretical the movements that attempted to acknowledge these truths.

Despite these encouraging historical moments, the church has a long record of abuse of women. It may appear difficult to find a usable past since everywhere we turn we see pictures of our unworthiness, guilt, and inequality. Further, if we take a once-and-for-all view of Christian revelation, that picture is hardly likely to change. Letty Russell is among those who believe that liberation theology offers women a way to find a usable past, although she acknowledges the difficulty faced in dealing "creatively and faithfully with tradition."[14] She argues that ample biblical evidence illustrates that a completed and therefore static view of revelation was a late addition to Christianity—a late addition that flies in the face of Jesus' promise of the Spirit who will lead people forward (John 16:13). Russell demonstrates that none of the so-called infallible traditions have actually been cast in stone by the

Divine. She illustrates her point by referring to the way in which the Divine was imaged in the Hebrew Scriptures. God is often referred to in female terms, and three of the most important ideas in Judaism are mentioned in the female: Shekinah (glory of God), Chokmah (pre-cosmic deity), and Torah (laws of guidance). The female nature of these ideas was downplayed over the centuries, which illustrates Russell's point that things do change. Therefore, feminist theologians may either change them back or look for new ways forward. She says, "The heresy of our time is not that of re-examining the Biblical and ecclesial traditions. It is the refusal of the Church to hear the cry of oppressed people and to speak and act on behalf of liberation for all."[15]

It would appear that by the time of Jesus, patriarchal thinking was firmly in place. An illustration is found in the figure in Proverbs 8, who may be identical with the Logos of Christian Scriptures. In the Hebrew Scriptures she is female; in the Christian Scriptures she becomes male. Ruether points out that this change suggests an ontological connection between the maleness of Jesus as the historical person and the maleness of the Logos as a male offspring and disclosure of a male God. At the time messianic hope was also largely pinned on a warrior king who, given the culture of the time, was best envisaged as male. Therefore, salvation would be supplied by a Jewish male figure who sat at the pinnacle of an elitist hierarchy.

Jesus did not appear to accept such a scheme. He did not evoke Davidic kingly hopes; rather, he praised the lowly and outcasts for responding to his message while the reigning authorities stay encapsulated in their systems of power. Further, he did not envisage the kingdom as otherworldly, nationalistic, and elitist.[16] He saw it come on earth when basic needs were met and people could live in harmony. In this new community we would not be servants but brothers and sisters, thus replacing the old idea of patriarchal family with its inevitable inequalities (Matt. 10:37–38; 12:46–50; Luke 8:19–21). Jesus also declared that God was not speaking in the past but speaking now to challenge the law and its outdated, life-stifling interpretations (Matt. 9:10–13, 18–22; Mark 2:23–28; John 4:10; 8:4–11). Ruether argues that once we see Jesus in this light, we find a Redeemer for women. She says,

> Jesus, restores a sense of God's prophetic and redemptive activity taking place in the present-future, through people's experiences and the new possibilities disclosed through those possibilities. To encapsulate Jesus himself as God's last word and once for all disclosure of God, located in a remote past and institutionalized in a cast of Christian leaders is to repudiate the

spirit of Jesus and to recapitulate the position against which he himself protests.[17]

Women can find a Redeemer because their experience in the present can be seen as valuable in the redemptive process. Ruether argues that the disciples had not expected such a denouncement of their messianic hopes, so they began to turn Jesus into a doctrine rather than risk embracing the event of eternal liberation. She suggests that this process begins in Luke, where Christ becomes a timeless revelation of divine perfection located in the past. The risen Christ does not live on but ascends into heaven; therefore, access to Christ is through the official line of apostolic teaching, which only men can administer. She is not entirely surprised by this since "the Gospels are written from the perspective of converted betrayers, disciples who know they had been unable to hear the radical character of his message of abnegation of power in his lifetime."[18]

We should not be taken aback that the church continues the betrayal of Jesus by using his name as a means of power and domination over other people. A large step toward this continued patriarchization, as Ruether calls it, came with the establishment of Christianity as the religion of the Roman Empire in the fourth century. The political power that Christianity gained from this enabled it to reinstate the concept of the Messiah with its roots in kingship. The Christian emperor with a Christian patriarch at his side could be seen as representing the establishment of Christ's reign on earth.

That was a devastating move, particularly for women. God had chosen the emperor, so hierarchy must be part of the divine plan. With the introduction of Aristotelian biology in medieval scholasticism the hierarchy became even more securely established with males seen as normative and representative of the fullness of human nature. Women, on the other hand, were viewed as defective physically, morally, and mentally. Woman's inability to represent Christ became an unchangeable mystery that emanated from the metaphysical plane, and the male normativity of both heaven and earth was well established. Given Ruether's investigation, we are left to wonder whether Christianity has anything to offer women and whether women can once again find Jesus.

Ruether is not pessimistic. She thinks that there is enough in the tradition that can be liberated to turn patriarchal interpretations on their heads. She views the task as that of struggling with Jesus for the transformation of the world, beginning with an option for the poor and oppressed. For her, Christology does a number of things apart from calling us to seek justice. It also makes us recognize the interconnected nature of injustice and to admit to the role of dominant ideologies in the perpetuation of injustices. Most important, we have to admit that the fullness of the Christ event is connected with the coming of the realm. The latter is plainly not here, and so Christology has a partial feel, that is, the qualities that we call Christlike in the life of Jesus are still to come to fullness. Jesus did not fulfill all the expectations nor did he establish a church that could simply live in the glory of that victory. The expected Messiah has not come, and to pretend that he has helps us to be numbed to injustice and suffering in the here and now. Ruether claims that Jesus can act as a sign of messianic blessedness to those who wish to see him that way, but rightly understood, he is one among many who signal that another order is possible—what we call the realm of God.

Ruether was one of the first theologians to make connections between Christology and ecology. She bases this on her belief that there is one covenant for the whole of creation and not just for human beings. Pointing to the Hebrew Scriptures, she shows how the prophetic-messianic tradition promises peace and harmony in nature as well as justice lived in all areas of life. It is no coincidence that the Jubilee includes more than human beings. Everything has to be given a chance to recover itself: human beings from debt, animals from over-work, and the land itself from overuse. Nothing is to be placed in a situation of enslavement to another, but all must have some respect accorded it. Ruether argues that Christianity has developed in such a way that the spiritual person is set against the natural world. This tragic move has meant that a hierarchy has been developed that extends from heaven down to the lowest creature on the earth and mandates all kinds of prejudices and social injustice. Ruether illustrates in her book *Women Healing Earth* (1995) how women from the Third World are providing the most sustained challenge to this pernicious way of thinking. The ways in which women and the earth are connecting for their mutual survival demand a radical rethinking of dominant ideologies, not least in theology.

A Relational Christ

Elisabeth Moltmann-Wendel is another who is hopeful that the Christian tradition has enough within it that is savable. For her, the stories about Jesus and women are less androcentrically edited than the rest of the Gospels, and she feels that here we see something of the true dynamics of Jesus. Once we move away from Jesus as the supremely powerful miracle worker, we see that the power that makes us whole is our own. Moltmann-Wendel agrees with Heyward (see chapter 5) that this power is experienced mutually; therefore, we do not effect our own salvation in an exclusive sense. She shows the importance of mutual experience by illustrating that the stories of women are quite distinct from those of men. The men come to Jesus with questions and discussions while the women feel and relate.[19] However, by the time of the second generation of Christians, Jesus has lost his earthly, sensual, touching character, and "the Christ" is a set of cerebral beliefs.

Moltmann-Wendel illustrates how this process developed with reference to the story of the woman with the hemorrhage. In Mark's tale she touched Jesus, but when the story is retold in Matthew, only Jesus' mind was touched (Matt. 9:21). Moltmann-Wendel sees this as the workings of patriarchy that have already split mind and body, giving higher status to the mind. She shows that the idea of power is already being distorted in the Gospels. Jesus exercises his power through loving and relating (Mark 10:45), and the women do the same (Mark 1:31; 15:41). But the men are concerned with who should be first (Mark 10:37).

The stories of the crucifixion also highlight the changes taking place. In Mark the word *theorein* is used to describe what the women were doing at the cross. It means "perceiving," "understanding," and "knowing" in the same sense as "knowing the signs" as used in John 2:23. It is not an intellectual activity but means that one is totally caught up in and affected by the events. It signals that the women were being wounded by what they were immersed in witnessing. By the time Luke tells the story, he uses *theasthai*, which suggests they were simply onlookers.[20] The sense of mutuality in relation is lost by the time the tale is retold by Luke.

Moltmann-Wendel argues that an alternative tradition in Scripture has been buried by patriarchy, but can be recovered. She suggests that the stories of Jesus and women show a love that transcends class, race, sex, and moral value. Discipleship flows from this love and is not an act of obedience but a form of communication that produces community. We read:

> But the God whom Jesus proclaimed is rooted in the matriarchal Sophia tradition. Jesus' way of addressing God as Abba and the sisterly non-patriarchal order which he depicts are in accordance with this picture of God. If the gospels illustrate the disastrous move from mutuality to hierarchical power then the writings of Paul present us with a piece of male theorizing. A personal experience is made the basis for a universal valid theory, his own experience of guilt becomes our own experience of God.[21]

God becomes separated from guilty humanity, and Paul's guilt assists him in developing an idea of atonement that had nothing at all to do with Jesus' death and his ideas about salvation. By doing this one at the same time escapes the radical nature of the message and avoids the call to be involved. The mutuality and challenge of love are lost. This has serious consequences for everyone but particularly for women. It becomes extremely difficult for women to claim their full humanity and right to divine power within this kind of patriarchal and guilt-ridden Christianity, resting as it does on the fall of humanity from a state of perfection instigated by the actions of a woman.

Moltmann-Wendel is aware of the difficulties but is hopeful that women can change the system and humanize the patriarchal God, just as Jesus tried to do. The images are there in Scripture, but most of all "we have the images in us, in our bodies, in our self consciousness. We develop them among us. . . . We are the church and if we reject the pernicious heresy of the separation of the spirit and body . . . we shall be in the thick of the process which cannot be restrained any longer."[22]

Like Heyward, she is declaring that Jesus encourages us to take our humanity seriously and in so doing transform the world by the sheer outpouring of our *dunamis*. (*Dunamis* is the raw, innate, and dynamic power that is our divine birthright. It is the energy that propels us to seek justice in relation with others. It is a life-transforming strength into which we grow.) We can bring God back from the clouds and the impotence that implies and make the "Kingdom of Mothers" in this world by the radical nature of mutuality that produces right relation and justice.

Mary Grey fires a warning against viewing redemption as simply justice: "Redemption seeks to transform the world at a deeper level than do the movements for freedom and liberation—yet it must include them."[23] Redemption carries with it more than social implications, although these will manifest. Our passion for justice increases our participation in the divine creative ground of our existence. As we become more like God, God will become more tangible in the world as the One who unites feeling, energy, and action. While involved in our own self-awakening and development, we are also in relation to a profounder process. We become linked through our developed awareness with a cosmic energy and attain visionary powers that enable us to prevent threatened disaster. Grey realizes this happens in books more easily than in life because we find it hard to transcend the categories of spirit and matter that have been imposed upon us. She feels frustrated in her attempts to find meaning since under patriarchy the concept "I want does not exist."[24] The deep and transforming nature of relation is more often lacking than it is experienced, but when it does occur, it is "sheer grace which cannot be elicited or grasped by will alone."[25] Hence we can only really grasp the idea of intentionality and will commitment at an intellectual level. Mutuality in relation is left to our feelings, which can know more deeply than our minds ever can.

We must strive for this depth of knowing despite Sharon Welch's assertion that our sanity is preserved only by blocking levels of sensitivity and mutuality; if we did not do this, the pain would be too great.[26] We have to be passionate enough to take up our cross and bear the result of mutuality. The concept Grey is seeking is one "which includes a dynamic flow of passionate energy, capable of being nourished between persons, through sexual relations or friendships of which sexuality is a dimension, but also in other ways because it is the fundamental creative and healing energy of existence. It is also the very ground or truth of existence because it flows from God."[27]

For Grey, Jesus shows how growth in connection can present a radical challenge and lead to transformative action. She illustrates that Jesus himself had to move toward this understanding. She suggests that he had three distinctive periods in his understanding of salvation.[28] The first suggests a young freedom fighter who views everything with urgency. In Luke 4:18–30 Jesus appears to be identifying with the task of Isaiah 61:1–2, creating liberty for the captives and freedom from oppression. There is emphasis on powerful external influences with salvation being something that happens to people. The second phase shows Jesus realizing that salvation involves both the inner person and the outer person; therefore, he is able to accuse the Pharisees of outward show (Luke 11:39). He also seems to realize that salvation involves self-knowledge (Luke 11:52), which leads us to seek forgiveness (Luke 15) and to live from the level of justice and compassion. Grey says the third phase shows Jesus developing the redemptive task in global terms.[29] We see too that the values of the realm of God are at odds with the values of the world (Luke 18:17). There is also the suggestion that conversion at an individual level is not enough. What is required is a conversion at a deep and cosmic level. For Grey, the redeeming power of Jesus lies in his ability to discover and make manifest "the divine source of creative, relational energy in a way powerful enough to draw the whole world with him."[30] Jesus' own vision of this is clearly stated in John 17:20–26 where God is pictured as a relational being.

If Jesus' life was based on power-in-relation, then the understanding of his death needs to be consistent with that. If he suddenly surrenders his power to God, then the basic tenet of mutuality is overthrown. An alternative understanding of sacrifice needs to be found. Grey suggests that we view it as a "total response in mutuality to justice-making in a particular situation."[31] It is a passion for justice so great that it causes us to offer ourselves totally in a way that could be called sacrificial. It is not passive, and there can never be a suggestion that suffering is good in an intrinsic way or that we should actively pursue it. There is no good in suffering, but it is a risk we take if we make ourselves open to the possibility of power-in-relation. Grey believes that claiming power-in-relation is actually claiming resurrection power in the world.[32] We are no longer simply believing in something at an intellectual level but are participating in a living energy that manifests in our lives and therefore in the history of the world. By our living this resurrection, endless creative activity throbs through the world with huge potential for change.

EROTIC REDEMPTION

This same power is called erotic power by Rita Brock, who uses the term to illustrate that she is dealing not with abstract concepts but with our deep desire for union with others. The power does not allow us to be safe and conveniently conventional in our world. It empowers us to look for justice and commits us to building that justice. Brock is convinced that erotic power redeems both us and Christ, since it does not descend from on high but it is the product of grace, which we find in the heart. She says,

> Heart is our original grace. In exploring the depths of heart we find incarnate in ourselves the divine reality of connection, of love. . . . But its strength lies in fragility. To be born so open to the presence of others in the world gives us the enormous, creative capacity to make life whole. Yet such openness means that the terrifying and destructive factors of life are also taken into the self, a self that then requires loving presence to be restored to grace.[33]

It is in finding the heart that we realize how we have been damaged and our original grace has become distorted. This memory and the anger we should feel at this memory open us to our deepest passions, and it is here that our erotic power lies. It is a power that is enhanced by relationship, not by control and dominance. Erotic power is wild, uncontrolled, and beautiful. This wild heart saves us from the sterility of living purely in the head. Erotic power and embodied knowing involve subjective engagement of the whole self in relationship.[34]

Brock suggests that Christ is an image of shared power that increases in the sharing rather than a once-and-for-all event in the person of Jesus. She criticizes liberation theology for emphasizing the historical Jesus as a revelation of divine will since she does not find it beneficial to think of him as a heroic Savior who defies authority. She says that most liberation theology still operates with a sin/salvation model of atonement, even though it understands sin in a societal way instead of individual action.[35] Brock also criticizes Ruether for seeing Jesus as prophetic because he morally transcended patriarchy. She maintains that biblical prophets are heroic figures who have very private relationships with God and proclaim them against all the odds. They do not usually suggest any kind of community interaction, and they perceive the world as a proving ground for the prophets' personal message and relationship with God. The world is also a place where he can show his unilateral power. Jesus as prophet is liberated and liberates others. Brock criticizes this view because it makes people victims to be acted upon and Jesus the hero who speaks and acts for the people. Although Ruether says Jesus is redeemed too, Brock says she does not show it.[36]

Brock may be making the mistake of seeing the power to redeem as a linear concept. It may also be seen as a circular notion. A prophet may be receiving revelation from God, but this same Deity can dwell in people and so the revelation comes from within the people it is meant for. In this way it is not only circular and interactive; it is also nonhierarchical because it is open to all who have eyes to see. The world in which Jesus was active and the people that he met certainly called forth his power and vision.

Brock sounds a warning note to those trying to reconcile feminism and Christianity. For her, the reconciliation between the two lies not in Jesus as a hero declaring a world in which women may participate but in the realization that "divine reality and redemptive power are love in its fullness."[37] She is adamant that basing Christology on a historical figure is a mistake because it confuses the concept with the phenomena. We need to see the saving events of Christianity in a wider context than the person of Jesus.

In Brock's opinion the shift in feminist Christology has been from seeing Jesus as the locus of redemption to viewing him as the focus of faith. She illustrates this with reference to the healings in Mark's Gospel. The miracle stories have been neglected by Christology except by conservatives who have used them to show Jesus' dominance or by liberals who give them allegorical meanings. Brock insists that they should be seen as normative statements about the nature of the Christian community and should be understood as the outcome of connectedness through erotic power. They show what is possible when we live from the level of connection and not from the level of power-over.

They show our divine power. They also "point to the political implications of disease and to the social-psychic nature of much sickness. They present inclusive and sophisticated metaphors for understanding the relational nature of sickness and suffering."[38]

The mutuality and connectedness that Jesus uses through exercising his erotic power stand against systems that cause disease. The exorcisms as much as the healings are statements against the societal causes of illness. The biblical picture of exorcisms is not one of personal sin bringing about possession; therefore, personal penance is not the way to overcome it. Further, exorcisms are performed by Jesus not because he has the power to forgive but because he has experienced the same demons and has been empowered by his own experience to release others. The temptation stories show a wounded healer who understands vulnerability and inner oppression. Brock claims the same is true of us: once we name our own demons, we have the power to help others claim their erotic power. In this way erotic power is not only political but also relational.[39] How intimate this power is and how physically based it is can be seen by Jesus using breath, spittle, and blood. Miracles do not require the bestowing of hierarchical power or ritually pure surroundings. They require connection (Mark 6:6). Even the healer needs healing, and Brock uses the anointing of Jesus to illustrate this point.

Brock continues this theme by focusing on the women at the cross who also illustrate the power of connection. They "represent a caring patience that can be wounded but not denied."[40] She suggests not that they are perfect disciples but that they persist in the midst of brokenness despite their fear. They return to anoint the body in an effort to bring healing in the face of total destruction. For Brock, the resurrection highlights how the power of connectedness can live on in others despite Jesus' physical absence and the trauma of the terrible manner of his death. The concept of resurrection is a testimony to the healing power inherent in the world.

Christo-Politics

Elisabeth Schüssler Fiorenza approaches feminist Christology in a slightly different way from many of her feminist sisters. She sets out to explore the theoretical frameworks of various discourses about Jesus and not to write revolutionary biography or a postpatriarchal Christology. Feminist movements seek to intervene in the struggle over the control and commodification of knowledge, and they try to keep the knowledge of radical equality alive in the eyes of the disenfranchised.

This is a hard struggle in the reality of global systems and requires global analysis. Schüssler Fiorenza believes that theology has to play its part or religion in general and Christology in particular will be a dangerous weapon in the hands of those who wish to reinstate conservative and oppressive regimes. Conservative political forces use religion as a cover for arguments that will lead to their advantage. Fundamentalists employ the modern media while rejecting many of the political and ethical values espoused by the modern democracy.

"The political-religious right," states Schüssler Fiorenza, "claims the power to name and define the true nature of biblical religions against liberation theologies of all colors and geographical locations. Its well-financed think tanks are supported by reactionary political and financial institutions that seek to defend kyriarchal capitalism."[41]

These right-wing groups have portrayed emancipated women as signifiers of Western decadence or modern secular atheism and have also presented masculine power as divine power. In such a context women must not give up the power of naming by respecting conservative claims to ownership of the texts. Feminist theologians should seek to destabilize the center by speaking both the language of our intellectual theological fathers and the dialects of our feminist sisters. Feminist theology is a political practice not only for personal change but also for structural change. As so many women collude with the structures, feminist theology has to address itself to tackling the self-hatred of so many women as well as confronting cultural disrespect for women.

Schüssler Fiorenza uses the term *kyriarchy* rather than patriarchy to describe the system as she sees it. She thinks that "the hermeneutical center of a critical feminist theology of liberation cannot simply be women."[42] It has to account for other oppressions and for women as oppressors. The emperor/lord/master/father is the ruler, and this legitimates the intellectual and cultural framework that exerts social control. The Catholic Church and modern capitalism are modeled on classical kyriarchy with a person at the top casting dictates at the lives of millions. This term *kyriarchy* comes from the Greek city-state where we see the tensions between radical democratic ideas and the kyriarchal reality. It goes without saying that democracy is an illusion under such a system, although that illusion is tenderly nurtured since it suits those in control to appear open to people-powered change.

SOPHIA—CHRIST REDEEMED?

Schüssler Fiorenza is aware that most Christologies to date are in one way or another products of kyriarchal thinking. Liberal enlightenment

Christologies have glorified this model with Jesus seen as the greatest man who ever lived and is also defiant, autonomous, and beyond all human limitations. This has in reality meant that we are under the spell of male white supremacy since the white male is always cast as the hero in our culture while Jesus himself has been somewhat bleached over the years and also appears as the white hero.

It would appear beyond doubt that classical Christologies were shaped by imperial interests, which can be illustrated by highlighting the words used in various Christological definitions. For example, the Council of Chalcedon made its declaration in the name of the church fathers and the emperors Marcion and Valentinian, and it used two separate Greek words to describe incarnation. The one least used was *enanthropēsin*, which means to "live among" or "have human form." The one used the most was *oikonomia*, which means "household management" or "law/order/administration." Therefore, the mystery of the incarnation in this usage is best described as the mystery of Jesus' order/law/management/economy. The mystery is that of kyriarchal power. This is further highlighted by all the exclusions that the council proclaimed. The council defined itself as the holder of power and meaning, of no less than divine power and meaning. The true nature of Jesus was defined as *oikonomia* and therefore confirmed the givenness of the imperial order and intolerance of diversity. Thus, Chalcedon was political.

Schüssler Fiorenza uses the *ekklesia* of wo/men as a counter argument to kyriarchal definitions (wo/men to show we are not one group but fragmented by structures of class, race, etc.). To articulate *ekklesia* shows that an alternative system that is fully inclusive and just can be found. It also calls for the hermeneutic of suspicion as we try to assess "the kyriarchal effects of christological articulations on the lives of wo/men in the global village."[43] This critique shows up kyriarchy and the politics of meaning. Schüssler Fiorenza tries to engage with various Christological discourses in order to intervene in and subvert the politics of meaning. She claims the women's movement can offset the oppression of kyriarchal Christology by developing emancipatory praxis. When we are immersed in action, we become able to subvert dominant meanings through face-to-face encounters. However, she warns that even a relational Christology, grounded as it is in action, should guard against being too personal. It still needs to be articulated in sociopolitical terms because the modern liberation question is no longer, Does God exist, but what kind of God are we proclaiming in a world of oppression? How does God liberate? Through the changing of sociopolitical systems more than by miraculous intervention.

Feminist Christological hermeneutics are oriented to a liberation praxis and therefore hold biblical stories responsible for shaping public reality. Exploration of a biblical text begins not with the text itself but with a critical articulation and analysis of the experiences of women. How have the texts affected reality, and how does that have an impact on the lives of women? Schüssler Fiorenza is aware that none cause more problems than those that have led to a theology of the cross. In the last century Elizabeth Cady Stanton pointed out that Eve, the founding mother of sin, and a male Savior were intertwined problems for women. Mary Daly took up the point by showing that Eve, the cross, and the sacrificial nature of Jesus encouraged women to be scapegoated and to remain passive about that scapegoating. Elisabeth Moltmann-Wendel and Mary Grey have tried to re-image atonement and redemption in such a way that they will speak to feminists positively. Moltmann-Wendel sees the cross as a paradoxical symbol of life while Grey wishes to reinvent atonement as at-one-ment and suggest relational mutuality. Although Carter Heyward no longer sees the cross as anything other than a political tool, the means by which many died in order to try and subdue a people, it has no redemptive, atoning function. Further as Brock points out in *Journeys by Heart,* Christologies that are about submission "sanction child abuse on a cosmic scale." By ritualizing the suffering of Jesus, kyriarchal power protects itself from those who may otherwise object to their own suffering. By making his death nonpolitical, the status quo can preserve itself. However, if we see his death as political and image the resurrection as the presence of Jesus "going before you to Galilee" (a place of political dissent), then the cross does not support kyriarchal power but actually undermines it and makes it look to texts for its own validation.

Schüssler Fiorenza's approach is to search for Divine Wisdom. This is a difficult task since traces of her are buried in masculinist Christological traditions. Nor should we be lulled into thinking that even if we find her, the lot of women will be improved. The Hebrew Scriptures make her more visible and are positive about her, but the lot of actual women was not always a happy one. The Christian Scriptures, particularly the Johannine literature, highlight a stage when Jesus is given the attributes of Sophia. Some of the earliest traditions of the Jesus movement understood Jesus as the prophet of Sophia who was to make the realm of God available to the poor and marginalized. As a child of Sophia, he also made the message experientially available to all through ministry and miracles. One of the earliest Jesus sayings states that "Sophia is justified by her children" (Q Luke 7:35), which signifies that Sophia is with all her children and is made just in and by them.

The statements that have been hijacked to proclaim Jesus' atoning death can be seen in a different light as confirming that Jesus was the prophet of Sophia, for example, "Therefore also the Wisdom of God said, 'I will send them prophets and apostles, some of whom they will kill and persecute'" (Luke 11:49).

This suggests that the earliest reflections on the nature of Jesus were Sophialogy, not Christology. Schüssler Fiorenza wants to argue that Jesus does not close the Sophia tradition by being the last and greatest—that is a contradiction of the tradition. Rather, he opens it further. He stands in a long line of Sophia prophets, both men and women, who have been killed for the message they bring. Their deaths were not willed by Sophia; indeed, they are lamented (Q Luke 13:34). This lamentation is directed not at all the Jews but at the governing authorities. Thus, Sophialogy helps overcome the anti-Jewish tendencies inherent in traditional Christology.

Many scholars think that Jesus replaced Sophia, but according to Schüssler Fiorenza, close examination of the texts shows that Jesus is handed the attributes that Sophia always possessed (Matt. 11:25–27). Therefore, he received them from her. The Father God does give Jesus knowledge, but Sophia, who was present at creation with God, already has the qualities that Jesus inherits from the Father. Schüssler Fiorenza explains the exclusive father/son language as the drawing of boundaries by the early communities. The baptism of Jesus confirms the view that he was a prophet of Sophia as she descended upon him like a dove (the gray dove was the symbol of the immanent Sophia while a turtledove was a symbol of her transcendence: Philo). Like Sophia, Jesus found no dwelling place among human beings and so was given one in heaven (Sophia: 1 Enoch 42:1–2; Sir. 24:3–7). Similarly, they were both exalted and enthroned, assuming rulership over the whole cosmos (Isa. 45:23; Phil. 2:6–11). The Christ is understood in terms of Sophia as the mediator of the first creation and as the power of a new, qualitatively different creation. This understanding of Sophia allowed Christianity to have a cosmic agenda, to believe it could change the world.

Elizabeth Johnson also develops her Christology in terms of Jesus-Sophia. She is convinced that the early church used many of the traditions about personified Wisdom in order to come to an understanding of who Jesus was. She asserts that it was only after he had become identified with Wisdom that he was understood as the only begotten Son. This signals a slight difference between the theories of Schüssler Fiorenza and Johnson. Schüssler Fiorenza, as we have seen, has no desire to view all the attributes of Jesus as the last word. For Johnson, the identification of Jesus with personified Wisdom does a number of things. It illustrates the importance of everyday living in the unfolding of God's realm, and it offers female metaphors as part of the divine process.[44] It also makes inclusion the central element of salvation. Those who are usually excluded are counted as friends, accepted, and loved, not simply tolerated or, worse still, forgiven. Jesus, as the child of Sophia, gives hope for the establishment of right relations across all boundaries.

For Johnson, the stories of resurrection illustrate how Sophia rises again and again in unimaginable ways. The gift of life cannot be overcome even by extreme torture and death. She will rise. The disciples are then commissioned to make the inclusive goodness of Sophia "experientially available."[45] It could be argued that Christianity is a resurrection faith only when this occurs. It is sadly true that Christianity has not always been concerned with spreading experiences of empowering goodness and inclusivity but has gloried in its own ability to define and therefore manipulate the Christ. As Johnson points out, asserting that Sophia was in Jesus defuses any sexist claims as well as claims to religious exclusivism. Personified Wisdom is at work all over the world and in many different traditions, and so Christianity can no longer claim special revelation. Sophia is also inherent in the world and demands a far greater ecological awareness and striving for balance and right order in the natural world.

Feminism has moved the Christological debate a long way from Jesus Christ, only Son of the Father, but has it really moved so far from Emmanuel, God with us? I do not believe that it has. Feminist Christology encourages us to become more intimately involved in a circular dance of cocreation and coredemption, one that is less concerned with the destiny than with the journey itself, a journey that involves all of one's being.

What at first appeared to be a simple shift in the language debate has shown itself to be a fundamental reevaluation of the Divine in the light of women's experience. It results in the affirmation of life itself, the body, passion, and mutuality. The insights of feminist Christology make it very hard to return to the worship of a God who demands suppression of our own divine, erotic power. It also makes it impossible to see Christ as the still point in a turning world who guarantees redemption. The feminist Christ is far too passionately involved to make any such dispassionate and controlling claims and guarantees. The feminist Christ knows the pitfalls only too well. However, with Jesus-Sophia there is hope that the forces for life will rise and rise again in the real stuff of people's lives and in the most extraordinary ways. Feminist Christology is full of hope that the world will be transformed rather than vainglory that all has already been accomplished. Christ-Sophia rolls up her sleeves to enter the struggle and encourages us to do the same.

5

QUEERING CHRIST

Queer bashing for Christ has unfortunately been quite a popular sport throughout Christian history. It has taken various forms—from individual beatings in the street to inquisitions and vicious church documents dealing with the "homosexual problem." Generally speaking, the churches have always been less tolerant of homosexuals and lesbians than society at large has been. They have done their best to influence society in the direction of intolerance. During the witch-hunts when so many women forfeited their lives to superstition, gay men did not escape. Many gay writers insist that the derogatory term "faggot" is a sad reminder to us of how thousands of gay men also died in the flames, used as the faggots to get the flames of execution under way. This cannot be proved as the source of the usage, but we do know that gay men were consigned to the flames.

Christian history displays a terrifying tendency to equate the heretic, Jew, infidel, and witch with the sodomite. Indeed, the word had this general usage for quite some time. The sodomite was the one who could threaten the social order by his or her otherness, that is, his or her inability to conform to the norm, which was white, male, and Western. Another term commonly associated with homosexual practice, "buggery," has its roots in this theory of nonconformity and heresy. It is a term that originates with the eleventh-century Bulgars, a Manichaean Christian group who practiced nonprocreative sex. They were declared heretical, and a derivative of their name used to signal threats to medieval society. During the latter half of the twelfth century, Europe became conformist, and it was common for orthodoxy in belief to be linked with certain sexual practices. That was a time of very detailed manuals (penitentials) about sexual sin with confessors asking very inquiring questions in order to establish that orthodox belief generated orthodox sex. The penitentials seem to spend a disproportionate amount of time dealing with homosexuality. They are very detailed documents that set out penances for different types of kissing, which discriminate between the active and the passive role and take into account whether the penitent is a monk or layperson. Where there is an age difference between the partners, the older one receives the harsher penance. The ultimate is the flames of the stake.

It is very interesting that this threat to the social order should be portrayed in sexual terms with the homosexual eventually being viewed as the ultimate threat and destroyer of civilized virtues. There seems to be an unconscious understanding that once those who rule society can control the physical expression of its citizens, then it has a tightly governed and nonrebellious society. The perceived naturalness of certain bodily actions regulates the social structure, which in turn literally comes to embody dominant values. The natural differences and roles of each gender take on symbolic boundary meaning, which was certainly the case in the medieval Christian world. The church has always understood that the body and the experiences we have through it are very powerful, and to this day it attempts strict control. The homosexual is the societal outlaw and to be feared.

Bernadette Brooten makes the point that Paul's declarations against homosexuality were based on this same understanding. She claims that he realized homosexual, and particularly lesbian, love would set the social order on its head, based as it was on sexual hierarchy. People literally learned their place in society by the sexual role they were molded into. It was a largely heterosexual arrangement, although older wealthy men could have young male lovers who were often from the servant class. Brooten contends that Paul believed so strongly that the end of the world was close at hand, he did not wish to present a challenge to the existing social order.[1] This attitude is evident in his approach to slavery and may also be the case here.

The situation today is not much improved in some places. The Christian right is violently homophobic. Its followers display bumper stickers proclaiming "Kill a Queer for Christ." Stalwarts such as Anita Bryant claim that homosexuals are no better than murderers and should be executed. Jerry Falwell encourages his followers to "stop the gays dead in their perverted tracks." It would be convenient for those who are not members of the Christian right to cast the blame for this blatant bigotry elsewhere, but this is not so easily done. The Catholic Church has also led an attack on homosexuals, although it sees itself as carrying out its pastoral duty toward them. There have been many unhelpful Vatican declarations. For example in 1986, the Vatican banned Catholic support for any organization that did not condemn homosexuality. In 1992 Cardinal Ratzinger issued a statement declaring that it is perfectly acceptable for homosexuals to be discriminated against in education, housing, jobs, and welfare so that they do not get the feeling that their lifestyle is being encouraged. He said that one would try to limit the activities of a virus; therefore, one must contain the homosexual from polluting the church and society. That was followed by the papal document *Veritatis Splendor* in which homosexual orientation was referred to as intrinsically disordered while homosexual activity was seen as constituting intrinsic moral evil and placed in the same list as genocide. While Vatican documents are condoning institutional homophobia, they are doing nothing to condemn the increased amount of violence that the gay community is suffering. As Catholic young people carried banners through the streets of Boston proclaiming "God Hates Fags," a deafening silence was heard from the Catholic hierarchy. The Congregation for the Doctrine of the Faith helpfully points out only persons who are open about their sexuality suffer discrimination. The policy of "don't ask, don't tell" that has worked so well for the clergy over centuries is obviously being recommended as a universal practice. In other words, Christian people are being asked to deny an essential part of themselves.

All these statements, we must remember, are to demonstrate that one is a true follower of Christ, to identify the boundaries between the insiders and the outsiders, the saints and the sinners. They are based on a certain understanding of Christ against which the logic of the arguments is correct, even if the murderous desires are despicable. The Christ who can be easily manipulated to suit these purposes is the Christ of dualistic metaphysics. This is the sanitized Christ, the One who required a virgin birth and yet more, the immaculate conception of Christ's mother, to shield Christ from too much fleshy reality. Robert Goss highlights the dangers of such a position: "The more that Jesus the Christ was Hellenized, ontologized, spiritualized, depoliticized and ecclesialized, the more the human person, Jesus, was neutered."[2]

The virgin birth, which was a very late addition to the Jesus stories, was a sure foundation on which to build an antisexual theology. Coupled with it was the notion of self-mastery, which Christians inherited from the Hellenistic world. They might have inherited it, but they really got carried away in developing it. Self-control became the sign of a real Christian, and that was control over the body. Augustine was very perturbed by the fact that his sexual organ could move by itself with no permission to do so from him. He pondered on sin as rebellion against

God, and he could think of no greater example of rebellion than the body that refused to obey the mind and the spirit. Therefore, for him, sex had to be the original sin and the gravest of sins that could be committed. Purification of desire through which the body once more came under the control of the spirit was to be the aim of Christians.

It went without saying that the Child of God was born without libido, and he was always in control of every part of his anatomy at all times. Therefore, by implication, those who could not control their passions were seen as almost idolatrous. The fact that sex is required for procreation exercised the minds of most of the early theologians. Even Luther could not find it in his heart to suggest that sex might in that case be a good thing. He is merely able to say that within marriage, and for the purpose of children, God winks at sex. Augustine was adamant that unless sex was for procreation, it was a damnable offense, and even then it demonstrated the body's rebellion and so had to be practiced with as little pleasure as possible. Along with many of the church fathers he thought that sex made men feeble-minded, they lost their rationality and spirituality, and so they should avoid it when possible.

As Goss illustrates, this mind-set gave tremendous power to men who were perceived to be living a celibate life[3] because they were seen to be emulating Christ and Christ's purity. The notion of the passionless Child of God has laid the bedrock of an at times heartless/passionless clergy and church. This asexual Christology was added to a very literalist reading of the Genesis story and made a powerful cocktail in the homophobic assaults that the churches have carried out over the years. According to a literalist reading of Genesis, normative humanity is heterosexual. According to Augustine, any heterosexual sex that took place in Eden was sinless since it was totally under the control of the will, passionless, and with no pleasure. However, due to the sin of the woman, passion entered the sexual equation, and that downward slide distorted humanity, ending later in a total abomination before God, the sin of Sodom. God's passionless procreative pair have been totally obliterated in this most abhorrent of sins, which allows pleasure without procreation. Men lose their rationality and abandon their God and with no good outcome—children.

Theologians addressing the deep-seated prejudice that exists in church and Scripture did not begin with advancing a gay Christ. Instead they concentrated on explaining the most homophobic texts and showing how they could not possibly underpin homophobic church dogma and practice. However, like most biblical criticism, it had limited effect, and some turned to developing a theology to deal with this issue. "Queer theology" is a generic term for a theology that speaks for a whole range of people outside the heterosexual main-stream—gay, lesbian, bisexual, and transgender. It is considered radical in its condemnation of the heterosexism and exclusiveness underlying other theologies. It grew out of liberation theology, the movements for civil rights, and the AIDS epidemic. The latter made it imperative that a devastated community find a theological voice, one that gave dignity to the not yet dead and rest and respect to the departed. (It was extremely difficult to find priests who would carry out funerals of AIDS victims or would pastorally counsel the grieving part-ners, many of whom did not have long to live.)

MUTUALLY EMPOWERING EROTIC CHRIST

Coming as it does from a tradition of liberation and influenced by fem-inist theology, this theology airs many of the same assumptions. Carter Heyward was among the first from the gay and lesbian community to develop a sustained Christology (I hesitate to call it systematic because of the negative images that the word conjures up). In the beginning she claimed her work as feminist and not lesbian. Only more recently has she made it clear that her Christology could not be separated from herself, her grounded being, her most intimate self, her sexuality. Her work is a very good place to start to find the queer Christ. Although she does not claim to have uncovered such a Christ, she does provide the foundations for others who claim they have.

As a feminist theologian, Heyward believes knowledge is based in experience. Her starting point for seeking to understand God is taking human experience seriously. She says, "We are left alone, untouched, until we choose to take ourselves—our humanity—more seriously than we have taken our God."[4] That means in her case taking her lesbian identity as a starting point in the creation of theology. She clearly explains why lesbian feminists have bothered to be involved in theol-ogy at all by saying, "We do not 'do theology' for the sake of 'doing theology' but rather because we who experience God moving within, between and among us believe that we must try to articulate what it is that we experience, in order to point to and lift up the presence of God here and now and in order to live and speak in God, through God and by God rather than simply about God."[5]

The emphasis is on experiencing God as a living reality, not as a plausible abstract concept. Theology lived by women is not about sys-tems of dogmas, doctrines, and categories, but is rather "a revelation of a living God whom we believe to be Godself defiant of all static, rigid categories and concepts. Feminist theologians cannot accept any dogma or theoretical concept in and of itself—that is, outside the context of in what ways it enhances and supports human life and women's lives in particular."[6]

The traditions have to be tried in relation to women's experience, and if they are crushing, not liberating, they have to be discarded. They have to be declared blasphemous and idolatrous because they lie about the nature of God and limit the unfolding of the Godself. This is not a task to be done alone since lesbian feminist theology is born from community and is about seeing who we are in relation to others. It is largely about relating—to ourselves, to God, to others, to the world.

In the introduction to *Touching Our Strength: The Erotic as Power and the Love of God* Heyward emphasizes the importance of relating to the creation of theology. Here she tells us that to come to the point of being able to write theology, she had to ground herself, to situate herself in her embodiedness through touch, smell, taste, and memory. The memory included those she had cared for and the battles that had been fought and were being fought both personally and internationally. She had to spend painstaking time and playful time with friends, and she had to make love, for "if I had not had a precious woman to caress my lusty flesh and bring me open not only to her but to myself and you,"[7] she could not have written a justice-seeking, embodied theology. This is very far removed from the days of ascetics, hair shirts, and denial of the body, but it is a logical starting point for lesbian theology.

It is essential to experience as good, and by so doing to experience oneself as good, what has been used to condemn one. Virginia Mollenkott asks, "How does a fundamentalist who believes she is essentially depraved become transformed into a person who knows she is an innocent spiritual being who is temporarily having human experiences?"[8] The answer is through experiences that she would call mystical, which were mediated through her body and those of loved ones.

As we explore Heyward's thought, we should have a clearer idea of what relating means. It is not simply saying we agree with Jesus and looking to his achievements as sufficient for salvation. Heyward says, "Jesus did not do it for us. Jesus' life does not spare us the need to live our own or to discover ourselves in relation to God. Jesus has shown us the way."[9] In a very real sense it is correct to say Christ is dying, Christ is rising, and Christ is here again in our lives through the revelation of our being and our actions in the world. What a powerful view this is. Is it not doubly outrageous when uttered by a lesbian? Such a statement does not devalue the cosmic power of the God but declares supreme faith in the immanence of that same God. It also perhaps encourages faith in the cosmic eternal elements of the human being.

Heyward suggests we need to stop viewing redemption as an act of God lifting us above ourselves, "a process of divine deliverance from the human condition."[10] Such a picture suggests that we should have eyes only for God, thereby detaching us from our world. This approach, she feels, is quite wrong since it detaches us from our most fundamental experience of human life—relation. We need to realize that this fundamental experience is God. We should not flee it; instead, we should embrace it. As we will see, "cocreative" for Heyward also means "core-demptive." Heyward expresses the relational nature of God beautifully when she says, "Humanity was born in the yearning of God / We were born to share the Earth."[11]

Here we see that if God loves us, we are needed, since "a lover needs relation—if for no other reason, in order to love."[12] A loving God can never, in Heyward's view, be an isolated and totally autonomous being who takes joy only in being adored.

God's creative power is the power to love and to be loved. Heyward declares it was this incarnate, loving, dynamic, relating God that Jesus made visible and that the church lost. She thinks that in the development of Greek Christology the ultimacy of the voluntary character of the divine-human covenant was lost.[13] To preserve the unity of divinity and humanity in Jesus, the Council of Chalcedon compromised the possibility of a voluntary union between a human Jesus and the divine God and opted for a hypostatic or essential union of the two natures.

Heyward believes that Antiochene Christology allowed for voluntary union and regrets it was superseded by Chalcedon, thus eliminating Jesus' human choice. The implication was that the possibility of free relation to God was replaced by the idea of inner union, almost an inner compulsion. Greek metaphysics crushed voluntary activity.

As the only begotten Child, Jesus was the only One who could achieve this union. The rest of humanity had to rely on God's grace. Heyward says, "For Jesus history was the realm of righteousness. For Christians earth became a waiting room for some other world where the righteousness achieved by Jesus would be fully revealed. Jews worked for the Messiah, Christians waited for the parousia."[14]

The acceptance of such a doctrine changed the emphasis on justice. Instead of being something people worked for, it became something God granted as a gift in the form of natural justice. It was not important to love your neighbor and our world, but crucial to love God, who was above both. Heyward is not interested "in the God who batters like a ramrod through the priestly pages of Leviticus and on into the misogynist diatribes of Jerome, Martin Luther and John Paul II."[15] She is passionately interested in the God of John 15:9–15 who

tells us to love one another and in the God of justice in Matthew
25:31–41 who wants justice for women (Luke 6:17–27) and for outcasts
(John 4:5–26) and who is the God of sexuality of the Song of Solomon.
She is interested in the God that Jesus knew in the intimacy of immediate relationship, whom he called "Daddy" (Abba).

Jesus saw no difference between our love for our God and our love
for our neighbor (Mark 12:28–31). In our labor, our birthing, we need
to include others when bringing into being the love and justice we
receive from God. We are laboring to create a new life based on mutual
love, one in which "we are dealing with a real love for man for his own
sake and not for the love of God."[16] There can be no passive obser-
vance if we are to be in mutual relation. Nor can we merely convey
"truths" from one generation to the next. We have to burn passionately
with a desire for justice, which is love of God, and be open to its unfolding nature.

Heyward is convinced that this is what the life of Jesus showed us,
and she embarks on a task she calls "imaging Jesus." It is a process of
expressing something about reality, of expressing a relation that we
know already between ourselves and what we image. Re-imaging may
mean letting go of tradition. One such letting go is realizing that Jesus
really matters only if he was human and if we view his incarnation as a
"relational experience."[17] Heyward believes it is a crippling mistake to
see Jesus as a divine person "rather than as a human being who knew
and loved God. It is crippling because it prevents people claiming their
own divinity." She does not deny the possibility of incarnation. If God
is a God of relation, then incarnation is bound to be not only a possibility but a desirable necessity. She says, "I want to re-image Jesus
because I see in what he did the human capacity to make God incarnate
in the world, a capacity no less ours than his."[18] She is not devaluing the
reality of incarnation but exposes the limits of exclusivity. By re-imaging
Jesus, she also re-images human beings by realizing the amazing power
and relation lying dormant in human nature. Jesus' relationship with
God is no longer seen as one of an obedient, adoring, and impotent
child but as "a growing child to a parent, whose power is appropriated
in friendship by the younger generation, organically, in such a way that
the maturing Jesus is able to baptize the world with God."[19]

Although the Gospels tend to imply Jesus' innate and complete
divinity, Luke hinted at its growth when he wrote, "And Jesus increased
in wisdom, in stature and in favor with God and men" (Luke 2:52).
There is the suggestion that Jesus was involved in the process, not
simply dragged by an overwhelming inner compulsion. Heyward does
not wish to deny God's parenthood of Jesus but wishes to re-image

beyond genetic terms and therefore as the source of power in which Jesus was grounded. She goes on to say, "It may be equally appropriate to image God as Jesus' child, whose growth in the world Jesus facilitates."[20] If Jesus' claim to divine parenthood is through claiming divine power, then he is quite correct in saying, "Anyone who does the will of God that person is my brother and sister and mother" (Mark 3:35). Anyone who claims his or her divinity is related to Jesus. In this way Jesus makes it quite clear that he is not speaking abstractly but is concerned with relationships between people and their empowerment from what they know as God.

Once we really value Jesus' humanity, the dualistic gulf between humanity and God is breached. It becomes possible to assert that our own humanity can touch, heal, and comfort the world and in so doing strengthen God. At the same time it becomes apparent that a God of love is as dependent on us as we are on her. She is vulnerable and can die when we refuse to be creative, loving, and liberating.

Heyward therefore re-images divinity as something we grow toward by choice and activity. This shift requires her to look critically at the notions of authority and power. She is anxious to move away from the idea that authority is something that is exercised over us by God or state and to come to an understanding of it as self-possessed. Heyward notes that two Greek words are used in the Gospels. One is *exousia,* which denotes power that has been granted. The other is *dunamis,* which is raw power, innate, spontaneous, and often fearful. *Dunamis* is not granted; it is inborn, and Jesus claims this authority. That is why Jesus could not answer his interrogators. They were not speaking the same language because they were interested in authority while he was concerned with power. And he could not be understood by those who wished to equate authority with religious and civil government.

What was new about Jesus was his realization that our *dunamis* is rooted in God and is the force by which we claim our divinity. It is not something that other people have; it is something that we have in the here and now. It is not something that others give us the authority to exercise; it is something that legitimizes our actions. By acting with *dunamis,* we, just like Jesus, act from both our human and our divine elements. If we accept this power and form of relating, we cannot see God and humanity in opposition. We can overcome the suspicion of human power and initiative placed in our religious understanding by the story of Eve and her actions in Eden.

Heyward's approach also eases the eschatological tension evident in the Gospels. Sayings such as "I tell you solemnly there are some standing here who will not taste death before they see the kingdom of God come with power" (Mark 9:1) become clearer. There will be no external Second Coming. Some people will experience their own *dunamis* and power to transform in the here and now. They will manifest the realm of God in their bodies and by their actions. If Jesus is God, then we cannot go and do likewise, but if Jesus was moved by God to love and in so doing made God incarnate in the world, then we can make the time now. It means that we re-image the realm of God as a place of justice, love, and peace between God and people rather than a place of clouds and winged disembodied beings to be aspired to but not gained until after death. We have to re-image the realm as a place where the lion lies down with the lamb and the tools of destruction are changed into instruments of creativity. When human beings dare to acknowledge their divine nature through *dunamis*, this kind of realm is imaginable and must be made incarnate through radical love.

Radical love incarnates the realm because intimacy is the deepest quality of relation. Heyward says that to be intimate is to be assured that we are known in such a way that the mutuality of our relation is real, creative, and cooperative. We do not have to be friends, acquaintances, or sexual partners to experience intimacy. It is possible to see Jesus' ministry as based on intimacy since he knew people intuitively, insightfully, and spontaneously. The relation was so intense that both people were affected. The fact that much of his healing was carried out by touch highlights for Heyward his desire to relate and at the same time experience his own *dunamis*.

Heyward examines Mark 5:25–34, which is the story of the woman with the hemorrhage, and wishes to re-image it. It should no longer be seen as Jesus' power being diminished but as the woman's touch being a sign of her commitment to being empowered (healed). This intense, vulnerable commitment enabled the flow of healing between them. Heyward argues that *dunamis* in relation is divine power and affects the healer and the healed.

I would like to explore the point further by referring to the raising of Lazarus (John 11:1–44) as an example of *dunamis* and the part that love plays in its release. The situation is admittedly different in that Lazarus is dead and presumably cannot seek empowerment. However, Mary and Martha are able to act as the people committed to empowerment, while Jesus' love is witnessed by his tears. Relation was created and *dunamis* claimed, and the outcome was life where death had been. I would agree with Heyward that a relational understanding of Jesus' power is a truer picture than that of the imposition of divine authority for divine glory. It could be argued that the raising of Lazarus shows that philosophical debate and theological accuracy are not what make

God more fully understood. Rather, vulnerable intimacy creates life and reveals the face of God.

Heyward's re-imaging makes it clear that Jesus does not have exclusive rights to *dunamis*. He facilitates our knowing and claiming of God as *dunamis* through relation. He reveals to us "the possibility of our own godding."[21] Time and again people reject this and cling to conformity, and Jesus points out: "You put aside the commandment of God to cling to human traditions" (Mark 7:8). In his lifetime this rejection led to Jesus' crucifixion and led to the death of God, not because Jesus was exclusively God but because humanity rejected the possibility of its own *dunamis*. Heyward says the crucifixion signals "the extent to which human beings will go to avoid our own relational possibilities."[22]

There is a further denial of Jesus today by Christians who insist on his otherworldly sonship and divinity and, in the name of this exclusivity, condemn and marginalize people. I suggest that the extent to which we claim exclusive and remote divinity for Jesus is the extent to which we show our lack of faith and commit idolatry through turning Jesus into everything that he stood against, in other words, a false God. It is not helpful to view Jesus as a mediator between God and humanity since neither is far enough away from the other to need mediation. Using Jesus as mediator "bears witness to our own ongoing hesitation to claim our power, our dunamis, our capacity to make God incarnate . . . immediately."[23]

Heyward questions the wisdom of referring only to the last few days of Jesus' life as the Passion. She thinks it is necessary to broaden the term and realize that mutual relation involves one in living passionately at all times and in all areas of one's life. She argues that if there is power in relation, then there is pain in lack of relation. Jesus, while experiencing God so intimately, could not avoid the pain of realizing that God was denied and broken when relational power was broken. Jesus would not have to go beyond himself to see that he too doubted and therefore damaged this power (Mark 15:34). Heyward sees Jesus' death as releasing people, not because it was good, but because he refused to flee from it, thus showing how committed he was to his task. It is wrong to see Jesus' death as anything but unjust or to dwell on his suffering as a way to heaven. Heyward observes that "the notion of welcoming or submitting oneself gladly to injustice flies in the face of Jesus' refusal to make concessions to unjust relation."[24]

We should be angry about injustice and suffering, not accept them as blessings. Hard as it is for women and other marginalized people to do, we should view anger positively and allow ourselves to experience it. Perhaps this is one area in which the example of Jesus redeems as we see that his anger fed his power in relation; it did not diminish it. We should view anger as a positive alternative to self-doubt, depression, and a sense of helplessness. Jesus did (Mark 9:19; 10:14; 11:15–19; 12:38–40; 14:6). If we look at his anger, we find it is usually directed at injustice, nonrelationality, and misuse of humanity. If we get angry enough and keep our courage, perhaps we too can witness the reality of a new way, a realm on earth. Other gay theologians have expanded this theme, as we shall see.

Heyward does not go into great detail about the resurrection, but she does say that whatever it was, it did not remove or lessen the injustice of Jesus' death. She says it is possible to re-image it as a seed planted in the soil of Jesus' decomposition and harvested forever in his friends' subsequent refusals to give up intimacy and immediacy with God. After Jesus' death, his friends learned more deeply how to claim their own power because he was not there to do it all for them: "What began with Jesus and those who loved and were loved by him continues among lovers of humanity,"[25] or can if we will claim our birthright, our power. In this way Christianity is a resurrection faith when those who follow it preserve intimacy, power in relation, and passion.

Michael Clark, however, is convinced that we need to abandon ideas of resurrection in any form because they create the wrong picture. He says, "God is not an all-powerful vertical rescuer but is instead a horizontal co-suffering power, strongest on our behalf in our experience of (vertical) godforsakenness and insistent that we assume responsibility for justice."[26]

A God who will fix everything in the end is a cruel monster if God will not intervene now. This kind of God is of no use to persons in the midst of the AIDS crisis; this God makes their suffering worse. Clark does not see the need for miraculous intervention in the death of Jesus to validate his message. Jesus stands in a long-established prophetic line, and that is enough to validate him and his words.

I think it is clear that Heyward's model of viewing Jesus requires that we value human experience, since it is only through experience that we can god the world. Anything that denies human experience has to be rejected. Heyward points out that structures based on domination negate all of the above, both for the oppressor and for the oppressed, since no relation exists. There is a warning for church structure as well as civil and political structures. It is a warning shot fired by a doubly marginalized woman, who as a lesbian has felt the weight of oppression in religious and civil spheres. Heyward thinks that Jesus removed God from the future and the purely metaphysical realm and grounded divinity in action. (That was not a totally new understanding and one that was in keeping with his Jewish heritage.) Therefore, Christians should long not to return to a primordial state of innocence but to passionately engage in the liberation of human beings from unjust relation. In this way we are also involved in the redemption of God since when we act creatively and originally in relation to people and things, we enter into cocreation and coredemption.

People are afraid of their power and are then, according to Heyward, a godless people. She believes that "our fear has become the socially normative, religiously sanctioned preference to our passion. The destruction of humanity frightens us less than the co-creation of the world."[27] In our fear we commit evil through denying relationality, and in so doing we create the patriarchal God, the holy terror. We create the icon who is untouched by human love, the eternal King, the removed, judgmental, superior Being. "As a result of this we become crippled in intellect and reason ashamed of our own nature, cringing like a slave to an imaginary Caesar of the universe, fearful of what awaits us after death. . . . Can such a parody of man be anything but ultimately impossible for Nature herself to tolerate?"[28]

From Heyward's standpoint, nature cannot tolerate it. Our existence on the planet may rely on our Christological point of view. We have come to expect that our redemption will be handed down from above, but we need to realize that we are the saviors of God. Heyward suggests that we need to be aware not only of what we perceive is happening but also of what is actually happening. Everything is dynamic, and we find our creativity in that dynamism. Heyward's Christ is One who meets us where we are between the yet and the not yet and impresses upon us not so much the nature of the Christ but the meaning of who we are.[29] Therefore, the Christ is a friend who empowers, not a God who will manipulate. In this way, "God's incarnations are as many and varied as the persons who are driven by the power in relation to touch and be touched by sisters and brothers."[30] Because we are hesitant to claim our power, Christ needs to comfort us as well as give us confidence.

Heyward's Christology does not expound an unchanging, universal, absolute Christ but unfolds the face of Christ in various forms according to social, historical, and personal praxis. Her Christology is spoken not in philosophical language but in an ethical one. What happens is of more importance than true essences and elaborate descriptions. Heyward's Christ unfolds communally and therefore calls us to account through the experiences of the most trivialized and marginalized in the community. Most of all, Heyward's Christology is fully embodied, sensuous, and erotic, seeking vulnerable commitment, throbbing with expectancy and power.

Heyward is only too well aware that traditional Christianity will have difficulty accepting such an experientially based Christology, based as it is in lesbian embodiment. However, her lesbianism plays a large part in her Christological explorations because it is the ground of her experience of mutuality and her most embodied reality. She has since argued that the kind of mutuality she is expounding is most easily found between women. The power dynamics of gender do not make it an easy matter for men and women to find mutual empowerment in their most intimate acts. By placing herself outside that particular form of embodied inequality, Heyward believes she is able to experience different forms of power. From this lived reality, she reflects on the biblical Jesus and sees new possibilities. She is no doubt aware of her own advice: "Any feminist whose vocation it is to be a Christian needs to be aware also that her vocation is to be a prophet."[31] She must be a prophet because she must declare the alternate realities that she sees and imagines.

QUEER CHRIST

Many gay theologians pick up on the themes that Heyward outlines and develop them in a uniquely queer way. The term "queer" has been transformed from an insult into an empowering symbol of living out one's sexual difference in a homophobic society. Before the Stonewall riots on June 27, 1969, in Greenwich Village, the main aim of the gay community had been to fit into society. However, those riots, led mainly by drag queens and butch dykes, were a turning point in gay history. From them sprang a sense of self-worth, pride, and a demand to be accepted for difference and not despite it. There was to be no more extinction through assimilation but a proud outpouring of richness in diversity. The diversity is expressed graphically through body identity and actions, through what has become known as transgressive politics.

Simply put, transgressive politics is about refusing to play it straight. Transgression in the area of sexual expression means that one does not keep to the strict gender roles and the games that go with them. In other social areas it means acting in ways that are beyond the boundaries of what is expected. To be most effective, transgressive politics needs to go beyond the private and become a very public and communal display of resistance. An alternate community needs to be witnessed as having shape, or actions can be dismissed as those of crazy individuals. In terms of the church an alternate ecclesiology needs to be visible, one that is fully embodied rather than the product of abstract thought to which members comply. The embodied nature of the emerging transgressive church leaves it open to the possibilities of change as called forth by the demands of the situation. The embodiment also lies in the bodies of those who are breaking boundaries just by their very existence and the exploration of what may be possible through those bodies.

Many gay and lesbian groups, including ACT UP, OutRage, and Queer Nation, are acting both transgressively and prophetically through their confrontation of society and church. ACT UP has confronted the drug companies over their slow response to the AIDS crisis and their exploitation of those who hope for drugs that will lengthen their lives if not save them. Others have acted against the church. One member of ACT UP receiving communion at a New York cathedral crushed the host in protest against Cardinal O'Connor, who represented a silent church. That church has said nothing about action to prevent the spread of HIV/AIDS but still preaches against safe sex. Some ACT UP members viewed the crushing of the host as stepping too far while others saw it as following the lead of Jesus in the Temple. By turning over the tables and understanding the symbolic meaning that such an action carried, Jesus performed transgressive politics. He has then become a role model for those who feel that such actions are the only truly Christian way to act. They feel it necessary to act prophetically in a church that has lost its vision in favor of security and status quo power. The example of Jesus shows that direct action brings about change, so queer Christians are acting up. Jesus' actions in the Temple also legitimize anger for the gay community. He displayed what can only be called righteous anger, and the gay community feels it may rightly express this against the churches. To a certain extent, anger—and the search for justice fueled by it—encourages people to come out and to out others.

Coming out has always been seen as a political action, but only relatively recently has outing been viewed in this way. Queer Christians see coming out as an act of public witness, one that challenges homophobia directly. Some argue that not coming out damages others as it adds to the climate of homophobia. Coming out is seen as an action that has to be repeated many times and is a constant proclamation of one's faith in the queer Christ. It is an action that is quite unlike any other in the realm of liberation theology since it voluntarily embraces radical vulnerability, the essence of Jesus' message. In coming out, voice is actually given to what might otherwise not be known. Blacks, women, Latinos, or poor people are easily identified; in identifying who they are, it is argued that they lose nothing—the prejudice that they suffer is already in place. However, gays and lesbians may not be

visible, and in declaring themselves, they risk a great deal. To come out
risks lifestyle and at times life itself.

Queer theologians may be underestimating the significance of all
people outing their situation. It is certainly true that the poor are
already poor and women are already women, but a significant change
takes place when it is declared as a reality that deserves recognition and
a change of life on the part of the dominant. It too can be dangerous.
However, coming out is viewed as a Christic act since it goes against the
spirit of the age as Jesus did. Jesus loved even at times and in places
where the laws of his day forbade such expression. Jesus' love was considered disordered, just as gay and lesbian love is thought of, because it
was focused in the wrong place. For example, he healed on the Sabbath
out of love, he ate with tax collectors and sinners, and he stood up for
a woman caught in adultery. The Jesus who comes through in those stories is the One "who entered into immediate, shockingly unconven-
tional relationships with people, not evading the human encounter by
the choreography of the socio-cultural role definitions."[32]

The gay and lesbian community under the threat of AIDS has come
to learn the kind of loving that is urgent, risky, compassionate, and cel-
ebratory of life. Like Jesus, the community has enacted the realm of
God with each coming out, each embrace of another, every challenge
to law, and all the care of the dying. The modern-day Samaritans are
illustrating the same points that the first-century one so shockingly and
graphically portrayed. They are showing how the ritually unclean can
manifest the Christ more spontaneously than those tied into laws and
religious purity. This is not to suggest that members of the gay and lesbian community are perfect, but from their own experience, they are
also questioning the value of a perfect Christ since such a character
can sacrifice others to One's perfection.

Gay and lesbian communities suffer from many of the flaws that
they so often speak against, such as ageism, body perfectionism,
racism, and sexism, but queer Christians are aware of this and fighting
hard to overcome the problems. They are also attempting to make
space in which bisexual and transgender people can explain their own
theological understanding. The gay and lesbian community has
approached successfully the homophobia among gay and lesbian
people. This problem has claimed many lives because self-hatred is a
killer. The queer Christ instills self-love and self-worth in a way that the
straight Christ has never done and never set out to do. The heterosexual Christ controls gay and lesbian people through teaching fear and
self-loathing, just as the white Christ controlled black people. The
queer Christ releases people from the tyranny of the Bible and church

doctrine into a place where the celebration of diversity and loving connections can carry people forward.

Outing should be understood against this background. It is not a vindictive act carried out for pure malice but a political and angry action. Those who are outed have generally made antigay statements in the public arena. Such statements are viewed as aiding the homophobic climate; therefore, in a spirit of righteous indignation the individual is denounced. Queer Christians see this as following the example of Jesus, who would not tolerate hypocrisy and called the hypocrites to account. Outing has been controversial from the beginning, based as it is on making the lives of others into public spectacles. However, it is argued that through antigay statements, the lives of gay and lesbian people are diminished. Once the balance is considered, outing is seen as the lesser of two evils.

So is Jesus really thought to be queer? The answer is, on one level, a definite yes and, on the other, maybe. In the sense that the liberative praxis of Jesus releases gays and lesbians, then he is certainly queer. Many of his actions, as we have seen, can be the basis for transgressive politics, and his acceptance of people acts as an impetus for queer self-love. Some people argue that the love between Jesus and Lazarus was physical.[33] Others are comfortable with the idea that Jesus was physically at ease with Mary Magdalene and the beloved disciple as well. That is to say, he broke many of the boundaries of physical intimacy that were held to be normative in his day. Most agree that Jesus was a sensitive man who was not afraid of intimacy and knew how to love. Tom Driver[34] argues that Jesus was a shaman who was an agent of transformative power. He created luminal spaces from which to challenge society. It is perhaps in this way that the queer Christ speaks most loudly. He is on the edges along with the gay and lesbian community. He is in the in-between places; he is the outlaw. (In the United States homosexuality is outlawed in twenty-four states.)

Robert Williams states that "gays are by nature a highly luminal people. We live our daily lives in the luminal spaces between society's perceptions of 'masculinity' and 'femininity.' In our homophobic culture, we also inhabit the luminal spaces between respectability and criminality."[35] This can be a place of Christic creativity. It can never be a place of complacency and smug self-satisfaction. Many gay Christians are spurred into transgressive living because they live on the margins and realize that, however respectable a lifestyle gays and lesbians lead, they will never be on the inside. In many countries in the world gays and lesbians are one step away from criminal prosecution, social ruin, and even death. Why should they support the systems that make such laws through being model citizens? After all, the system will never support them.

Jesus: Unclean Friend

Queer Christology images Jesus as friend and lover. As a friend, he values the contributions and criticisms of his friends as well as taking into account the challenges posed by the queer life.[36] The centrality of friendship in gay and lesbian life calls into question the primary role of marriage in the Christian life and sometimes blurs the lines between friend and lover. The Christian right endlessly proclaims that the family is the backbone of a Christian society and, by implication, suggests that Jesus thought so too. However, according to recent scholarship, this does not appear to be the case.

William Countryman[37] has drawn attention to the fact that underlying many of the morality declarations and customs was an understanding of purity and property that we do not share. Jesus appeared to challenge the purity laws, pointing out that it is not what goes in or out of a person that is defiling but the intention behind the actions. Matthew stated that most strongly by giving a picture of Jesus eating with the impure and putting them ahead of the religious people of his day. He was unconcerned about contamination through touch and association and also brought into question the whole notion that certain people were unclean. By challenging the purity laws, Jesus broke down the barriers between people.

According to Countryman, Jesus also challenged the property laws on which contemporary marriage was based. Marriage was a hierarchical arrangement with the oldest male in the extended family acting as the patriarch, who literally held the power of life and death over all the other family members. Jesus challenged that in a number of ways. He said that his own family consisted not of blood relatives and the hierarchy involved, but of those who follow God—and he went on to call them friends. He declared that a wife was no longer to be seen as a disposable asset to be divorced at will; rather, there was to be equal partnership. By using the child as the ideal model for the Christian life, he turned the hierarchy right on its head. By granting equal status to women within marriage, Jesus was giving them equal status when it came to the "being robbed" stakes of adultery. As the law stood, the husband was considered robbed of his property if another man had sex with his wife. He could demand compensation and the death of his wife to avenge his honor. However, a wife, who did not own her husband, had no recourse in law if her husband committed adultery. By overcoming the view that people can be owned by others, Jesus challenged the law. Adultery loses its meaning since we no longer think in terms of ownership but regard each person as owning his or her own body. It becomes possible to see adultery more as a gift of oneself. Marriage is transformed from an institution with rigid rules that govern the bodies of those involved into a coexistence of equal partners who do not give up autonomy over their bodies. It is a friendship with body sharing.

Queer Christians who, in the name of Christ, have been denied access to traditional marriage are now, in the name of Christ, denouncing it as an outdated and slave-inducing institution that is not based on the teaching of Jesus. It becomes clear when the adherents of the religious right speak about marriage that they have another agenda, and that is control of women—and through them a tighter hold on advanced capitalist society. In a fascist document entitled the Family Protection Act introduced into Congress in 1981, women's access to sex education, contraception, abortion, and divorce are to be denied. They are to marry and stay at home to breed Christian children. The really interesting part is what is expected to happen if they do not: "Millions would be put out of work, multiplying minorities would create ugly turbulence, smaller tax bases would diminish the military's nuclear weapons stock pile and a shrinking army would not be able to deter potential Soviet expansion."[38] Fortunately, Congress did not pass this act.

The Christian family is to be the base for domination of economy and resources by the white right. While those who advocate the family are not all as fascist as that particular group, the realization that the family and how it is organized is a crucial element in any capitalist society is always there.[39] Queer Christians therefore welcome the accusation that they are a threat to the family; they would certainly hope to be.

Many queer Christians are modeling their relationships on friendship[40] because this eliminates any notion of ownership and emphasizes the equality to which they aspire. It also suggests that each person is calling out the best from the other by loving challenge and tender support. Because friendship in the West has rarely been equated with sex, some criticism has been leveled at this model, suggesting that it almost wishes to legitimize same-sex relationships by removing the overt sexual element. It would be fairer to say that in centralizing friendship, attention is being drawn to the fact that same-sex relationships can understand desire in a broad sense as the motivation toward justice and right relation.

Jesus, Sex, and Power

Martin Stringer[41] criticizes this emphasis on justice, believing that it
assumes all sexual encounters are in some sense sacred and highly intimate. He is honest enough to draw attention to this as a myth. He also
highlights that in doing this, queer theologians are in danger of rein-
venting the Christian arguments about the best way to experience sex.
He wishes to look at the way in which sex has developed under the
threat of AIDS in order to find a truer representation of the challenge
of queer sex to the Christian story.

Stringer maintains that people have had to develop sexual imagination because the emphasis, if one is to be safe, has had to move from
purely genital encounters to full body ones.[42] Through this transgressive engagement with one's body and those of others, a nondualistic
understanding of the body has emerged. In other words, the meaning
of the body is contained within it and not in some hidden place, nor
does meaning have to be imposed in order for there to be meaningful
interaction between people. Further, getting away from genitality in
pursuit of sexual pleasure has released gay men from the many power-
laden meanings associated with penis activity. They have found there is
less emphasis on performance and more on playful intimacy. Gay men
are also required to be more present to one another since they can no
longer rely on assumed sexual patterns, which can become almost
unconscious. This new pleasure seeking has brought many gay men to
a greater degree of mutuality, selfhood, and imagination. They have
come to learn that empowerment does not spring from power-over,
control, and rehearsed rituals. It lies in spontaneous, unself-conscious,
playful giving and receiving. Many gay Christians have come to a
deeper appreciation of the life of Christ through freer sexual expression in which they embody his spirit of self-giving.

Stringer likens this broader understanding of sex to sharing a meal.
Not all meals are sacred, and sharing food with one person does not
mean we have to forgo sharing with others. Sex can be shared in the
same way.[43] This understanding releases people from notions of ownership and could be argued to reflect the way in which Jesus himself
imaged friendship and body sharing. A literalist reading allows us to
point out that Jesus even encouraged others to share his body through
food after his death. Was this meant to be the sanitized and pious occa-
sion it has become, or a glorious, sensuous engagement with others
through the medium of food? A celebration of consuming one another
in Christ based on the memory of Jesus feeding others with his body,
emanating from his passion for them.

One element that queer Christology has reintroduced to the debate is the body. Queer Christians have celebrated their bodies in cultures that hate them. They have found self-worth and friendship through the bodies that in other times and places would be placed in the flames. This has set the scene for the body to be reflected upon as a crucial starting point for theology. It is strange that an incarnational religion such as Christianity has had such trouble placing a positive view of the body at the center of theology. Generally speaking, when the body has been focused on, it has been as something to be overcome or a vehicle for greater and higher values.[44] Both views—the body as a place of sin and the body as a symbolic representation of dominant values—have not served the queer community well. Therefore, a transgressive challenge has been issued. The churches are being called to embrace the flesh and learn through it the power of joy and mutuality.

Christ is seen as fully embodied, and queer Christians understand their sexuality as a force for seeking justice and connecting beyond the boundaries of their own skins and those of their lovers. Queer sex is pleasure oriented, which makes Christian ethics pleasure seeking within the broader context. The pleasure of which bodies are capable becomes the yardstick for measuring ethical actions rather than the self-sacrifice that Christians have been encouraged to endure. This requires an ethic of fair trade as much as one of sexual fulfillment. Those whose bodies are malnourished, poisoned, and withering due to exploitative economic policies and restricted access to medical care are removed from the pleasure that should be embodied in their lives. The embodied Christ cries out against this because he does not allow the promise of heaven to be sufficient reason for injustice to go unchallenged. The queer Christ requires the celebration of embodied life, and that in turn demands justice. Nor does the queer Christ allow one final and absolute imaging of his body. The embodied Christ is as varied as those who inhabit bodies. Queer Christology offers an embodied friend who revels in the ongoing discourse, loves the challenges, and celebrates the joy of connection.

6

CHRIST AMONG
THE SHAMANS

This chapter examines Christological perspectives from the women of Asia. I make no apology for concentrating only on the women. I made the decision because theirs is new and exciting work, which challenges the liberation matrix to the core because of their situations of sexism, racism, colonial intervention, and economic exploitation.

THE VARIETY OF ASIAN INTERPRETATIONS

The landscape of liberation that is viewed in this chapter is wide, covering writers from the Indian subcontinent, Korea, the Philippines, and Hong Kong. Although these women are often placed under the heading of Asian, this description is too general and shows us nothing more than geographical location. The reality is that they experience the world in different ways. What the West has defined as Asia includes more than half the world's population and contains seven major languages. Economic realities are also vastly different. Almost half of Asia is still under communism; in other areas there is advanced capitalism at its most rampant, for example, in Hong Kong. It will be interesting to see what happens to this tiger of capitalism now that it is under communist control. Asia graphically illustrates both dehumanizing poverty and glittering opulence. Further, the racial and cultural mix that we find gathered under this one title could not be richer. And the gap between Western and Asian mind-sets could not be wider. Asian and Western women have a great deal of decoding to do before they can begin to hear one another. The strength of women's theology is that it is willing to embark on that exercise rather than attempt to make all speak the same theological language.

Asia is a pluralist society in the true sense of the word, being the birthplace of many of the world's religions. Within this context Christianity is a newcomer and seen at times as the rather immature junior relative. Despite constant missionary attempts, less than 3 percent of Asia is Christian, and these Christians live in an environment where the alternative is not atheism or lack of religious practice. Asian cultures vibrate with alternate forms of spirituality, rituals, and festivals. Asian theologians, then, realize that Christ has to be understood through interreligious dialogue. Christianity did not arrive in Asia in this humble manner. Its arrival was triumphalist and crusading, and the intent of those who brought it was conversion of the indigenous people. That was beyond the experience of the people of Asia, who had for centuries experienced new religions in a totally different way. Generally, new religions were treated with respect and in return afforded respect to the older traditions. The coexistence led at times to the development of different forms of religion emerging from the dialogue of equality that existed.

Christianity was not humble enough and could not find it within its exclusivist construction to offer respect to the existing traditions. Christian imperialism wished to impose universal absolutes believing, as it did, that those who were being thus treated would in the end be grateful for having received true understanding. Such superiority of thinking did not apply only to religion. The peoples of Asia were seen as religiously, culturally, and intellectually inferior. As in the rest of the world, Christianity went hand in hand with colonialism and the exploitation accompanying it. This is not the whole picture since China and Japan, for example, resisted colonialism and were often the imperialist aggressors.

Asian women theologians have already exposed imperialism in the exclusivist approach to Christ and in the so-called inclusive approach. The former claims that the truth lies with Christ while the latter is far more subtle. The inclusive approach claims that good Hindus or Buddhists are in reality unconscious Christians or that their traditions carry within them the unknown Christ. This approach was at one time viewed as radical since it did not insist that others actually join Christianity but took comfort in the fact that Christ was at the center of their religion anyway. It was quite some time before the patronizing nature of this approach was exposed. Such an approach does not allow for real differences to be valued and explored. Asian theologians look on with some relief, and no doubt amusement, at theology in the West because its more liberal aspects have only recently arrived at the understanding that a pluralistic theology of religions is required in the world. Kwok Pui-Lan graphically highlights Western naiveté:

> We Asians have lived in a religiously pluralistic world for centuries and we have always believed that truth is more than a few propositional statements. In Western symbolic logic, the opposite of "A" is "Negation A," and the two must be mutually exclusive. The yin-yang philosophy in oriental thinking understands that "A" and "Negation A" are correlated, interdependent and interpenetrating. The Buddhist logic is even more radical for it insists that all reality is neither one nor many but is not-two (non-duality), in an attempt to overcome dichotomy in our thinking.[1]

The Christ of hypostatic union who sets up oppositional duality throughout the whole of the universe has a long way to go to even find a language with which to dialogue.

We can see that any talk of inculturation that involves rerooting Christianity in Asian soil is fraught with problems. This approach still assumes that there is a body of religious truth that needs to be adapted to the Asian context. Asian women are no longer willing to accept such an approach because it assumes too much that is not always helpful for them. This approach is uncritical of both the sexist texts and the core doctrines of Christianity as well as the patriarchy inherent in many Asian cultures. Asian women theologians are committed to creating theology from their own context using indigenous folk literature, traditions, and lived experience. They are open to the possibilities of exploring theology through poems, dance, and rituals, and they realize that in so doing they will be challenging basic elements of Christian theology.

The embodied memory that most carry of this new and exciting approach is from the Assembly of the World Council of Churches held in Canberra in 1991. Chung Hyun Kyung gave a plenary paper accompanied by drums, dance, and ritual—some of which was modeled on the *han-pu-ri* ceremonies from Korea. Within this embodied illustration she spoke of the need to create a dramatic paradigm shift in doing theology, one that allowed her pain as an Asian woman to be addressed. Asian women's theology is narrative in that it emerges from the ongoing story and is not rooted in the already told and fossilized universalist tale.

CHRIST—SHAMAN OF *HAN-PU-RI*?

Telling their story has deep roots in Korean culture, particularly in *han-pu-ri*, which comes from a shamanistic background. *Han* is a "root experience" of the Korean people because it signifies their oppression and the lump in their spirits that has ensued. They feel resentment because of the injustices they have suffered, and they have a feeling of helplessness and total abandonment. There is a deep desire for revenge in the sense of putting things right.[2] Women have experienced their own unique kind of *han*, moving as they have from more or less equal status in ancient Korea to a place of silence and second-class citizenship in modern times. Women in Korea suffer sexual violence as well as a wide range of abuses both within and outside the home. Many of the women who are sexually abused decide to kill themselves because of the culture of shame surrounding them. Christianity has not in any significant way altered the lot of Korean women, which is unsurprising existing as it does in a culture that is deeply affected by other traditions. This is not to suggest that Christianity would, left to itself, be the liberator of women because we have seen this is not always the case. Despite the fact that two-thirds of church attendees in Korea are women, they have not achieved their full rights. Many Korean Christian women are looking to their own traditions as well as Christianity to find a way toward liberation.

Han-pu-ri is one place they look. It is a ritual carried out by shamans who are usually women, and its purpose is to give voice to ghosts or people who have no other way of being heard. Once they have been heard, the source of their oppression has to be named, and action has to be decided that will overcome the oppressive situation. It is hardly surprising to know that a large number of the shamans and participants are women since this is one of the few ways in which oppressed women can get together away from the gaze of men and tell their stories. They speak to a listening audience who will then help them find ways to improve their situation.

Chung Hyun Kyung argues that women's *han* has to be the starting point for theology in Korea. In this way she is similar to other feminist theologians who understand the lived experience of women to be the place that all theological reflection has to start. The experience of women in Korea is unique to them, so the outcome of their reflection will be distinct. They have experienced oppression and resistance, that is, they have also acted as liberators. Both oppression and resistance require a process of critical reflection in order to untangle the webs of abuse that impinge on the lives of women. Therefore, reflection and critical engagement with tradition act as two more links in the creation of women's theology. (Many Asian women do not use the term "feminist" in relation to themselves and their theology because they see it as just one more Western construct that they do not wish to have imposed upon them.) Korean women also use texts in a radical way. They go behind the stories and beyond them to meet the community that exists in the written word. From their experience they know that what may be a liberating word for men may not act in the same way for women. They look for women in the text, and they view even their absence as significant. Korean women judge as good theology anything that liberates them from *han* and empowers them.[3] These same standards are applied to Christology: a good Christ addresses *han* and liberates.

According to Ahn Sang Nim, Jesus could not be anything other than a good Christ because he came to preach good news to the poor and women are the poor of the world. He is then their Christ. If we are in any doubt about this, all we have to do is to look at the genealogy of Jesus. There we see that he rejected the prowess that goes with patrilinear heritage and came solely through the body of women. His ministry is one that is involved with freeing women from patriarchal bondage. Ahn Sang Nim gives many examples of how this is done, all of which could be of benefit in other cultures. However, the one that is particularly interesting, reflecting as she does from her own background, is that of the woman who shouted to Jesus, "Blessed is the womb that bore you and the breast that you sucked" (Luke 11:27). In his rejection of this and his praise instead of those who hear the Word of God and keep it, Ahn Sang Nim does not see an insult to or devaluing of Mary. Indeed, she interprets this as the rejection of the notion that women are simply "instruments of succession for a family name," which seems to be their role in much of Asia.

By going behind the story and understanding that women's worth then, as now in her own culture, was seen in terms of childbearing, Ahn Sang Nim is able to look with new eyes at Jesus' response. Her conclusion is that Jesus is the One who values women's bodies and does not wish to see them used as sex objects, breeding machines, or fodder for industrial growth.[4] This interpretation offers a strong critique to traditional Christianity, which prefers not to address issues related to Jesus and the sexed bodies of others. It also critiques the way that some Korean men view the bodies of women as providers of comfort, economics, and heirs. Asian women were viewed as property to such an extent that they did not even have their own names. They were referred to in relation to the father, then the husband, and finally the son. For example, Mr. Park's daughter became Mr. Kim's wife and finally Dong's mother. Korean women were in this sense no-body; they had no name of their own. A Chinese example illustrates the point, although the same would be true in Korea. When asked if anyone was at home, a Chinese woman alone in the house used to answer, "No there is no one at home."[5] One of the tasks of Jesus the liberator is to give each woman a name by which she can be recognized and which she can call her own.

Although this naming process of Christ has a specific reality in Korea and China, it is also foundational in most theologies of liberation. Most groups that are developing liberation theology from their particular experience would agree that they are nameless but for the names of contempt that the dominant culture places on them, such as "nigger," "faggot," "whore," "slut," "spick," "gook," and so on. There is, it is argued, the upside of the naming process: blacks are strong and athletic, women are good at homemaking and factory machine work, Latinos are happy, and homosexuals are artistic. Why is it that even these so-called compliments seem threatening, as though they could be used to underpin oppression at the drop of a hat? The power of naming, when it does not lie in one's own hands, is dangerous, however innocent it may seem. True liberation lies in the beauty of proclaiming one's own name in opposition to a dominant culture that names for convenience and power.

Korean women do not start with Jesus as their namer; rather, they start with him as cosufferer. Imaged as the Suffering Servant, he is able to know their true feelings and empathize with them. This image seems to speak to most women theologians in Korea, wherever they are positioned on the theological spectrum. This model shouts loudly that domination is never right, and the women need to hear this message. They are also able to find meaning in their own suffering—not in the traditional way of supposing it will bring them rewards in heaven but by viewing it as redemptive for others, just as Jesus' suffering was said to be. There are always dangers involved in seeing suffering as positive. One runs the risk of sacrificing oneself into oblivion. Chung Hyun Kyung is aware of the particular dangers for Korean women. They have had a mixed message about suffering both from their own culture and from the colonizers. She fears that some may find it easier to accept the suffering servant role in the traditional sense because that is all they have ever known. They are encouraged to love Jesus and to suffer while he seems largely absent from their lives. Chung asks if this is the only model they know because it is reminiscent of their fathers, husbands, and lovers.[6]

Those who reject this model also find the courage to reject other relationships of the same kind. Their courage comes from the respect that they feel Jesus affords them and the sense of self-worth and dignity that this brings to their lives. This respect can be argued to come from the image of Jesus as Suffering Servant. He went through what they go through and came out with dignity. The women believe that they can do the same. This dignity provides hope for the future. They may be oppressed, but they are still engaged in redemptive praxis for themselves and others by envisioning dignity and freedom.

Chung Hyun Kyung points out that another title that has historically been used to oppress Korean women has been turned on its head by the women. That is the title of Lord. It was a powerful weapon in colonial hands as well as in the hands of fathers and husbands. However, women have come to understand it to mean that they are not subject to any earthly power since their only Lord is Jesus.[7] This is extremely empowering and allows them a degree of freedom that their earthly lords denied them.

We perhaps best experience something of the weight of culture when we consider the notion of incarnation. Lee Oo Chung points out that Korean culture has many heroes/holy people who become gods, usually after death, and so this is easy to understand. What is not so easy is the notion that God descended. Lee Oo Chung proposes that Koreans should understand the incarnation in terms of their own culture and adopt a bottom-up theology.[8] This provides Korean women with a powerful model since by following Jesus, they become like him, a process that builds up their self-esteem and raises them as high as the Divine.[9] The location of the Divine is changed from above, which encourages oppression and subservient behavior, to within, which gives dignity and divine meaning to individual lives.

This identification of the self and the Divine adds fuel to the fires of liberation, which is required on many fronts from colonialism, poverty, military dictatorship, and patriarchal societies. Women are putting their lives on the line to find freedom, and many are paying the ultimate price. These women are seen not only as martyrs but also as coredeemers with Jesus because of their gallant opposition to all that binds their societies. The blood of the martyrs is seen as fueling a resurrection hope. Others so outraged by the injustice of their deaths take up the fight and fill their shoes many times over. The fight for liberation is understood as a fight to liberate divine potential in the lives of women, not only to gain equal status in a sexist society.

The image of the defiant, crusading liberator is modified in some Asian theology with the idea of Jesus as mother, the mother who weeps for her dead children throughout Asia. This image challenges the laws of hierarchy and authoritarianism with a model of compassion and sensitive relationship.[10] Like those in the West who have used similar images, Asian women leave themselves open to the criticism that they sanctify motherhood in an unreal way. Not all mothers are caring, sensitive, and compassionate human beings. Many, some would argue due to the pressures of patriarchy, end up emotionally destroying their children in an attempt to control their lives. Many women are also reluctant mothers and empty their frustrations on the lives of their children. Another problem with this model is that it excludes those who have not been mothers or have no wish to be.

Park Soon Kyung, however, declares that Jesus is a symbolic female as he identifies with those who are hurt the most by society. In this context he is a woman Messiah,[11] similar to the black Christ put forward by James Cone. He becomes the One who, if he lived today, would be in the ghetto along with the lowest of the low. There could be a danger that people will begin to compete to see who is so lowly in society that Jesus would be bound to live among them. This is not meant as a flippant point but merely to illustrate that there are dangers in viewing Jesus as the One who dwells with the dispossessed, thereby giving them status. What happens if their position changes to one of relative affluence or if they are in some small part caught up in the web of exploitation, on the side of gain, that advanced capitalism makes it so hard to avoid? Where is Christ then? It has to be admitted that when people are totally dispossessed and marginalized, the symbol of Jesus with them in their suffering is a powerful one. The danger, I feel, lies in thinking that this is where one has to stay in order to remain with Christ. The question is raised whether Christ is most powerful among the poor and lowly. Then what are his place and power among the less oppressed? If he is imaged as powerful only when he is a marginalized victim, there can be no place. This seems a logical, but unsatisfactory, conclusion of claiming Christ for the lowly. (This theme will be explored in chapter 7.)

Perhaps the most powerful image of Jesus for Korean women is as shaman. Shamanism always played a positive role in the lives of women because it presented an alternative to the patriarchal realities of Confucianism and other religions. The shaman functioned as an intermediary between the spirit world of the ancestors and individuals or families. The shaman was able to exorcise demons and carry out rituals believed to change the families' luck. For this reason the shaman held a high position in society, and many shamans were women. Korean women are able to understand Jesus as a shaman because of his exorcisms and healings, which are familiar territory for them since as shamans they are exorcists and healers. Therefore, they are able to identify with him through their own actions. Jesus is identified as a big sister, just as the shaman is,[12] and not as "Lord of all" and "the only Son of God."

This female identification of Jesus is carried through the connections made between him and Kuan Yin. Kuan Yin is the compassionate goddess of the common folk who symbolizes relatedness, community, and suffering. She is a celestial bodhisattva who hears the cries of the world.[13] She is also a personification of wisdom and appears to people in need. Her suffering is connected with her wisdom and is seen as redemptive but in a radically different way from that of Jesus. Kuan Yin is a wise sufferer. She may walk a painful path because she sees the radical possibilities for change by so doing. This is a powerful message for women who often suffer for no good reason and have not believed that transformation should be the goal of their suffering. Korean women get a better perspective on their own suffering through the combination of their own culture with that of Christianity. They could become able to see their own position as that of transformative, redemptive suffering. The Korean imaging of Christ from below means that a hero or a mighty ruler would be an inappropriate understanding of the One who would be called Savior in the Korean context. Christ does not arrive triumphant in the lives of the oppressed but "emerges from the broken-body experience of workers when they affirm life and dare to love other human beings in spite of their brokenness. Workers become Christ to each other when they touch each other's wounds and heal each other through sharing food, work and hope."[14]

The sharing of these resources, particularly food, is another way in which the embodied Christ is understood. He is the grain since the grain gives them life. For starving people the greatest love and redemption bestowed by God are the next grains of rice. The traditional host, the so-called body of Christ, lacking in substance as it does and dispensed as it is from on high by the one with the power, is not a useful or powerful image in Korean circumstances. They require something that comes up from the ground and is shared by those who have no power, except for a communal will to live.

FILIPINO CHRIST

Turning now to the Philippines, we see a similar but distinct re-imaging taking place. The commonly held mythology about the civilizing influence of the conquerors is as prevalent here as in other parts of the world. The Spanish colonization was good for all, not least women whose status it raised. Naturally, this myth is now being explored and exposed, and we have a clearer picture of the role and position of women both after conquest and in precolonial Filipino society.

Mary John Mananzan[15] believes that the early ideas of God found during the precolonial period were female, with women being understood as solely responsible for the generation of children. There is no trace to be found of woman owing her existence to man, as in the Western myth of the rib. Even when men and women are seen as linked in the Godhead, there is no hint that the female aspect is less than equal. The female aspect of deity was understood as the most able to bring calm and restore balance.

The way that the Divine was seen to operate was reflected in society, and women had many rights and privileges. Both male and female children were valued, inheritances were equally divided, and both were given education. There were fewer sexual taboos, and unmarried mothers, for example, lost no standing in the community. They gained it since their power to procreate had been demonstrated, so they would be mates to have. This is not to suggest that the society was rampantly promiscuous. There were laws restricting excessive sexual activity and prostitution. Arranged marriages were the custom, but the woman did not take her husband's name. If she came from a well-connected family, he took hers. A Filipino wife was a companion who exercised authority in the household and had influence beyond it. Women were thought to have greater moral courage then their men and could be relied on to make good decisions in times of crisis.[16] Needless to say, women had some control in economic matters and were able to manage their own business affairs. However, women held the greatest power in the area of religion, performing all the rituals and communing with the spirits. Women were viewed as so exceptional at these tasks that when men did perform them, they often dressed as women.[17]

The Spanish had no respect for the people that their invading forces encountered, and as usual, they misrepresented them as lazy, unintelligent, sly, and morally corrupt. They had more respect for the women, seeing them as capable and more intelligent than the men, but that did not stop them from drastically altering their position in society in accordance with church teaching. The same arguments were used here as elsewhere in the Christian world: woman is weak, she is a temptress, and she is morally inferior. She had to be placed under the protection of men. To ensure that this protection could be fully exercised, most rights were removed from the woman, and she was placed under the control of first her father and then her husband.

Whereas precolonial religion had given greater freedom to women, the religion of the Spanish acted to underpin their subjection. The missionaries set up schools for young women, the earliest in 1696,[18] where the young women were domesticated through the imposition of devotion to Mary, the mother of God. She was to be their role model, passive and sexually inactive. Despite the model of chastity put before them, the young girls were sexual prey for clergy and laity alike. It seems that prostitution was introduced into society by the Spaniards, and many of the whorehouses were situated at the schools. Mananzan says, "On the pretext of putting woman on a pedestal as an object of veneration, patriarchal society succeeded in alienating her from public life, decisions and significance. She should henceforth be a delicate ornament of the home or the victim soul of the convent."[19] That was the gift of Christ to Filipino women, and they have to deal with this constructed Christ in their present-day struggles for freedom.

About 80 percent of the people live below the poverty line, and the vast majority of the poor are women. They suffer from the prevailing economic reality, and they believe they have no ability to change it. "They are today the Christ disfigured in his passion."[20] Many women identify in quite a passive way with Jesus' suffering. It can be argued that many Filipino women see the suffering and death of Jesus as ends in themselves, and they embrace the role of victim, viewing it as a positive religious experience. Yet others image suffering in a more radical form. They reflect on how Jesus had the strength to withstand it and conclude that this strength came through his sense of solidarity. This can be traced back through his life and can be seen in numerous acts of healing, teaching, and love. The death of Jesus as an act of solidarity inspires many Filipino women.[21] Women who were crushed under the weight of patriarchy are standing tall in solidarity with Jesus and their sisters. In this way they believe they are living salvation history with the assurance, pinned in Jesus' life and death, that the realm will come.

As with other Asian Christologies the emphasis is not on who Jesus is as much as where he is and what he does. Christology emerges not from theological debate but from the lived reality of believers and the process of liberation in which Jesus is felt to be active. In short, he is in the struggle, and he liberates. And as part of the struggle, he is involved in judging existing structures, and through the creative engagement of Christians, he offers new ways that bring freedom.

Filipino women do not find the maleness of Jesus to be a problem in their Christology. Born as he was, a male, he was in the best position to challenge the male definition of humanity and male privilege. He could offer a more effective challenge to men to change their ways. Yet the women have certain problems with culture. There have been many moves in liberation theology to develop more culturally appropriate models of Christology, models that grow out from the resident culture and thus sit well with it. In a patriarchal society this does not necessarily fill women with joy. Much effort has to be made to ensure that women are allowed to create a liberative space in their own culture before the cultural Christ is welcomed with open arms.

Virginia Fabella[22] believes that the historical Jesus plays a central role in the creation of Christology. Through his works and words, he showed what true humanity and divinity looked like; therefore, it is important to focus on him when seeking liberation in the present. As we have seen, there are any number of problems with this idea since the kind of historical accuracy that would be necessary to set out an exact way of being is not open to us. Further, to what extent does knowing how a first-century Jew acted help us to act now? The answers have to be generalized and open to a great deal of interpretation. Nevertheless, Fabella takes this path, despite her protestations about exploring the historical Jesus. It appears that what she means by the historical Jesus is One who changed things in the here and now. For her, Jesus' historical importance does not lie in accurately attesting to each action and saying, but it lies in our history. Although appearing to acknowledge this, Fabella still falls into the trap of assuming Jesus treated women in a radically different way from others of his time. Scholars now know that his actions were not as unusual as we previously thought. From what we have learned we know there may have been female teachers and possibly a female rabbi, and many wealthy women merchants who commanded respect and a large degree of equality. Some of these were also patrons of synagogues. We may assume that in that role they had some degree of input regarding the proceedings. Therefore, it could be argued that Jesus is portrayed as less than radical in his approach to women.

However, it is suggested that Jesus showed what being human meant, and this quality of humanness is needed if one is to enter the realm of God. To be truly human, one has to live in relation with others and exclude all power relations. Loving one another takes priority over worshiping in the temple, and serving others is more important than seeking and wielding power and prestige. This quality of humanness, which is open to all, is seen as a prerequisite of the realm. The emphasis on Jesus as the revealer of true humanness in many ways springs from the cultural setting. In Asia there is much interreligious dialogue but far more informal dialogue for life where people "share the life conditions, pain, risks, struggles and aspirations of the Asian poor (majority of whom are of other faiths or even of 'no faith'). . . . [It] made us aware of our common search for a truly human life, our common desire for liberation from whatever shackles us internally and externally, and our common thrust towards a just society reflective of what we Christians term 'the kingdom.'"[23]

If metaphysics and the infallibility of certain doctrines took center stage, such a dialogue would be severely hampered. The historical

Jesus who calls people to humanness bypasses such problems. Debates about the divine nature of Jesus are not allowed to hamper the transforming experiences for which people struggle as they act humanly. This has special significance for women in a society that has for so long limited their humanness through restrictive civil and religious practices. To demand human rights could be the Christological first step for many women. What is certain is that Jesus has no relevance for women if he is detached from their lives under the weight of metaphysics. He can never be static and is always open to modification by circumstances. However, this is a powerful element ensuring that Filipino women continue to include him in their struggles.

ORGANIC CHRIST

Ecofeminism is an important aspect of Asian theology and has Christological implications. Kwok Pui-Lan is one of the few Asian theologians to explicitly tackle the implications for Christology of ecology.[24] She is keen to show that she does not place ecology and Christology together because she is overfocused on Christ but because she believes that the West has been too anthropocentric.[25] This fault arises from the way in which Christ has been envisaged. Within the traditional view God sent God's Child to live on earth and save us all from sin and grant us life after death. The hidden message is that the natural processes of birth have to be overridden so that this divine human may be saved from the stain involved in the natural way of things. Further, we can be saved from the natural processes of decay. This is not a positive message for nature.

Kwok argues that this does not have to be the case because there is enough biblical evidence to create an organic model of Christ. Jesus called himself the vine and the disciples the branches, and the breaking of bread together is also an organic paradigm.[26] Kwok claims that an organic model of Christ makes plain the interrelatedness of human beings and the cosmos. If Christ is understood as the conveyor of wisdom, as some Western feminist theologians would wish, then from an Asian point of view much of that wisdom would concern the earth and the way it offers many challenges to the human race. Christ as wisdom, in the Asian understanding, sets a direct challenge to us to find ways to preserve and honor nature. Far from running from the evils that may be awaiting us in nature, we should embrace nature in loving and courageous solidarity.

Kwok offers an exciting way forward through her exploration of the organic Christ. This imaging of Christ allows us to move away from colonialism and anthropocentrism toward a more globally empowering sense of the Divine. It could be argued that Kwok is perilously close to the idea of the cosmic Christ, which was in truth no more than a religious colonization. However, the plurality of her background makes one suspect that this is not her intention at all. She is adding her own cultural awareness to largely Western pictures and changing the vista dramatically. Christ is understood in and through the stuff that Christians have been so encouraged to flee from. This leads Kwok to question the notion of the once-and-for-all revelation of Christ. Christ is rather epiphanic; that is, Christ is not one but many, and everyone has the potential to attain the status that Jesus attained. This view requires us to give up any dualistic thinking.[27] We are no longer separated from Christ by Greek metaphysics; the prototype that Jesus offers points us to the awesome reality that God is among us, in human beings and in nature.

Ecofeminism has been a dominant theme in Asian feminist thought for more than ten years. The work of Vandana Shiva has been significant; she shows how women and nature have been linked in a downward spiral under the weight of advanced capitalism. So-called development programs have done nothing more than introduce Western methods, and the Western idea of production for profit, into situations that were far more holistic and ecologically balanced. Women, who were at the center of this balanced approach, have been marginalized, and their wisdom, passed from generation to generation, is no longer heard. The consequences are tragic. While governments may, for the time being at least, generate more capital, women find it harder to sustain their families. As Kwok has pointed out, the wisdom that is Christ is being denied as women are dragged from the trees they are trying to protect and are told that trees are timber, resin, and profit. On the other hand, they sing that these same trees have sustained their ancestors for generations and would sustain them still if the saws could be stopped.

Chinese women may find the concept of the organic Christ a powerful one for addressing ecological issues, but Indian women develop the Hindu concept of Shakti. She is the underlying power of the cosmos, the one who represents the primal creative energy. The universe is permeated with Shakti and is a manifestation of her. This concept illustrates the relatedness of human beings and nature since it throbs in both. Ironically, this all-powerful and creative force, said to be present in women and to represent the true essence of Indian womanhood, is not respected in society at large. If it were, the position of women in Indian society would be better. Aruna Gnanadason[28] argues that this power has been submerged under patriarchal interpretations of religion as well as development models that emerge from the West.

She believes that the future hope for the whole of creation lies in the reawakening of women's Shakti. The Great Mother Goddess has to stir in the souls of women once more if the world is to survive and flourish.

Many Indian women are experiencing the reawakening of this spiritual path, and it makes them profoundly suspicious of traditional religion. They are questioning the status that religion has ascribed to women and are seeking ways to break out from the straitjacket of convention. It is a community-based undertaking since Indian women have no desire to make the same mistake of overt individualism that many Western feminists made. They wish to affirm the dignity and uniqueness of individuals as part of a community. In turn these communities and the individuals within them are actively involved in the critique of life-denying structures within their society. At a time when fundamentalism seems to be on the increase in all parts of the world, the women of India are demonstrating the strengths of pluralism. The fundamentalist surge has resulted in many restrictions placed on women, and so the celebration of womanhood that is part of the reemergence of Shakti is vital if women are to retain any sense of self. It is not entirely surprising, given the background of fundamentalism, that women are being drawn in numbers to the folk religions. They are almost entirely woman centered, and women are beginning to recognize their power to transform society.

GURU CHRIST—WOMEN'S SALVIFIC BLOOD

The women's movement in India is not a new phenomenon, emerging as it did in the 1940s in the Telengana peasant rising. Women organized themselves to fight against economic exploitation and bondedness. The movement was crushed by the British, and the women's movement did not emerge again in any significant way until the 1970s. The catalyst was the rape of a fourteen-year-old girl by two policemen who were not charged for the crime. Women were outraged, and protests broke out in all the major cities.[29] Many types of feminist analysis have informed the Indian struggle, and like other feminists throughout the world, Indian women have realized that their struggle involves more than just economic liberation. As women, they are also socially and culturally bound in a way that does not disappear with economic justice. For this reason many are focusing on religion because it has had a major influence in shaping culture and society.

Within this landscape Christology is a question for the 3 percent of the Indian population that is Christian. Christians are found mainly but not exclusively in urban and semiurban areas and represent many denominations from Roman Catholic or Methodist to Syrian Orthodox. All exist in a profoundly hierarchical and male-dominated culture. The traditional Christ has underpinned these tendencies, entering the scene as a colonial conqueror. Indian Christian women are engaged in a struggle against the triumphant Christ in an effort to ensure that the personhood of women is recognized and celebrated. Like their Filipino sisters, they begin with the personhood of Jesus, believing that this is the only way to demonstrate the power of universal salvation that lies with the Christ.

It is interesting that the historical nature of Christianity gives Indian women a starting point, claiming as they do that the life of the founder of Christianity has to be central to their reflections and subsequent actions. In the West, Daphne Hampson asserts that the fact of Christianity's historicity makes it completely unworkable in the future. She argues that we should know what is moral and just without having to refer to a man who lived in a different time and culture. By doing so we run the risk of not acting justly in our own time. She illustrates the point with the debate over the ordination of women. Those who claim that Jesus did not ordain women or count them among the Twelve are quite right; however, this argument from a time when the position of men and women was understood differently cannot be seen as just cause to exclude women today.[30] In addition, we face many problems today with which the historical Jesus had no experience and therefore cannot be expected to act as a role model. In these circumstances it seems dangerous to attempt to apply other texts and sayings to unrelated incidents. The tension remains, then, that Indian women as well as many other liberation theologians rely on the historical Jesus as a starting point, yet this is an unstable place to begin because of the problem of historical accuracy—history is never a fact; it is always an interpretation—and the cultural divide that is inevitable.

Monica Melancton hints at how some Indian theologians deal with the problems of the maleness and male identification of Jesus. This, she says, is part of the historical Jesus, but it does not mean that it is an essential ingredient of the risen Christ who is dwelling in the redeemed order.[31] This risen Christ transcends all particularities. In this way the maleness of Jesus can no longer dictate the femaleness of all women through time. He becomes the symbol of a new humanity rather than a model of gender enactments. Although this argument may be necessary within the Indian context, there are some problems with it. The notion that humanity is an androgynous mass underneath cultural overlays of gender enactment has been heavily criticized. Many feminist theologians, who have no wish to be shackled by the assumptions of essentialism, nevertheless argue that human nature is not androgynous and that many of the differences that we see displayed between the sexes have redemptive significance in themselves. There is always the danger that in claiming Jesus as the model of humanity, we have maleness yet again turned into universal ways of being.

From the perspective of traditional Christology this raises the question of the degree of Christ's humanness: Was he a man or not? If he was fully a man, to argue that he was fully human negates the place of female experience in humanness, and he did not know how it felt to be a woman. If he did somehow experience being both male and female, then he was either transgendered or not fully human. Being human is an experience, and that experience is in our day, and was in the time of Jesus, a gendered experience. However, this argument is not of primary importance in the Indian context where the landscape is one of rigid misogyny. Within that context emphasis on the humanity of Jesus rather than his masculinity is a crucial step forward.

The church in India has held in place the barriers to women's full participation and flourishing that are prevalent in society. Indian women are demanding that the churches should be countercultural in the way in which they believe Jesus was, and support them in their struggle for dignity in a patriarchal society. Their Christology emphasizes that Jesus was a Savior for women within their own patriarchal situation. He did not judge them by the standards of their society; for example, he did not condemn the adulteress, and he did not shun the Samaritan woman who had many husbands. He healed them, even when their illnesses would have made him unclean in the eyes of his society. Also, and crucially, he did not exclude them from what might be seen as the deeper things, such as his teaching and the revelation of his being. The women around Jesus, it is argued, actually understood his significance more easily than the male disciples did and tended to his needs more than his male colleagues were able to. They remained faithful when others fled. Jesus reached out to women and they to him in a mutual embrace of recognition and respect. Indian women theologians find this image most powerful.

They hope that this Christ will stem the tide of dowry brides, temple prostitution, and widow burning. Perhaps only this Christ can begin to balance the mortality rate, which reflects the fact that far more female babies die from neglect than should be the case. Many more are not even reaching birth since mobile scanners have made it possible for women in villages to know the sex of a child before birth and many are succumbing to the pressure to abort. Indian Christian women place their hope in the woman-loving Christ to raise the literacy level among women and to gain more stable employment rights for women. They also hope that rape and physical abuse both inside and outside the family will decrease. Christ will not do this through magic but through the realization that Jesus thought that women were human too and deserved the dignity and celebration attached to all God's creation. This message needs to be preached and lived in the Indian context.

Gabriele Dietrich[32] goes further and suggests a female image of Christ. She makes a powerful connection between the salvific blood of Jesus on the cross and women's menstrual blood. She claims that women's blood cries out, placing in front of us the many injustices that the female body suffers: the unwelcome abortions suffered because of poverty or social pressure, the despising of the female body coupled with its exploitation and the fear of women's strength.

Dietrich challenges the church that honors the womb for procreation but uses it symbolically to ban women from full participation in the life of the church.[33] We should realize that Jesus and women are joined through the shedding of life-giving blood. Both, it could be argued, struggle to be creative in a world that finds it easier to abuse than to love. Indeed, both also carry the pain of knowing that what they love could easily be destroyed. However, both will fight for what they love, even if that leads to death. The blood of women, menstrual and otherwise, is a sign of eucharistic community, understood as centered commitment and passionate action.

The women of Asia throw before us a vivid Christological rainbow, arising as it does from the tears of their diverse struggles. Their struggles have not historically been helped by the colonial Christ. As Christ meets the religious traditions and social situations of the women of Asia, Christ is slowly transformed. This transformation takes many forms—from the universal absolute of conquering armies to the unfolding healer in the midst of a broken community, from the Lord of all to the dispossessed peasant woman clinging to the grains of survival, from the unchanging Savior to the cries of the not yet saved, and from the blood of eternal salvation to the salvific blood of history.

If theology is to honestly face the realities of life and find a Christ who makes any sense within them, then it has to brace itself for an explosion similar to the original eruption into creation. The creative force innate in the universe is straining against the confines of Greek metaphysics and the power politics they so strongly support. This process is set in motion when faces look into others and marvel at the difference, yet celebrate the common gift of living presence. Asia, with its diverse cultures and manifold oppressions, is a fertile breeding ground for this next step in the life-giving revolution.

7

LIBERATING POWER, LIBERATING PRAXIS

The imperial Christ—the Messiah of metaphysical absolutes and attendant supreme earthly power—is dying. Despite desperate attempts in some quarters at resuscitation, this Christ is fragmenting and crumbling before our eyes. What, then, are Christians left to say about this figure they once declared as the only begotten Child of God, born of a virgin, whose sacrifice alone brings salvation to those who believe?

A Christ is emerging from the oppressed and the marginalized just as Christ did in the Gospels. Christ's face is as mobile and expressive as it was in the early accounts, and seen in different lights, Christ looks quite different. However, we also find that Christ can be recognized even after a dramatic transformation such as resurrection. It has been argued that this something is the true essence of Christ's divinity. This unchanging character makes Jesus of Nazareth the Alpha and the Omega, the beginning and the end of human existence and meaning. This explanation relies heavily on Greek metaphysics with its talk of essences and unchanging divine characteristics. As a feminist theologian, I wish to get away from such dualisms and suggest that what are recognizable and salvific, after the many resurrections and transformations that the Christ has undergone, are the power and the praxis. These are not qualities that Jesus Christ alone possesses, and they resurrect the Christ among the marginalized even when the church, along with society, is hell-bent on crucifixion.

In this chapter I hope to develop these points and to reflect on some of the strands that have emerged as Christ has moved through the byways of liberation. I also intend to ask, What happens now? What might conceivably be the next step in the liberation debate surrounding Christ? This questioning—and the answer I hope to move toward—is as contextual as the rest of the book. My context is middle class, educated, Celtic, Catholic, and female.

To make my own Christological case, I must contextualize not only myself, but also Jesus. How his world was and how he acted in it are two different questions, and we are able to answer the former more easily than the latter. For me the historical setting of the man Jesus rather than the historical Jesus is of importance for reasons that I hope will become apparent. Therefore, I will spend a little time making a few historical points that I believe to be significant. Palestine in the first century was largely made up of peasants, tenant farmers, and the urban poor with a small class of artisans, perhaps 5 percent, of which Jesus' father was one. There was an even smaller group of social elites, and at the other end of the scale, about 10 percent were destitute. It was a conquered land, and the Romans imposed both civil law and taxes. As long as the people adhered to both, the Romans allowed religious and civil matters to continue in the hands of the Sanhedrin. One can only imagine the juggling act that the civil servants and members of the Sanhedrin felt it necessary to carry out in order to maintain some degree of autonomy. They were often faced with people who did not feel that compromise was the better part of valor and instead wished to see Palestine stand up and fight.

The spirit of rebellion was often fueled by religious fervor. It would be quite wrong to suggest that Palestine had one form of orthodox Judaism. The notion of orthodoxy did not enter the Jewish consciousness until after the destruction of the Temple in 70 C.E. Even then it was a gradual process by which the Pharisees came to dominate matters of religious interpretation. We should also remember that most of Judaism was by that time existing outside Palestine, which may explain its push to compact orthodoxy. After all, displaced people often find it important to have their identity as a group recognized, and distinct religious practice is one way of achieving this identity. What one believes comes to identify who one is. Once the people of Palestine no longer had a land in which religion was simply a matter of everyday life, orthodoxy rather than praxis became of great importance.

We have always known that Judaism as it existed in Palestine consisted of a number of groups, but we now have come to understand the influence of the Greek-speaking world both outside and inside Palestine. There was far more diversity in the world that Jesus inhabited than we originally supposed; thus, we cannot be as quick, as once we were, to attribute unique approaches to Jesus in matters of religion. Christians cannot use as part of their argument that he was Christ his nonorthodox approach to Judaism. There was no real orthodoxy to measure him against. This is a significant point in our own day when the Pharisaic desire for ordered belief systems seems to have taken hold in many Christian churches. It is extremely encouraging to know that orthodoxy, in the time of Jesus, was less important than living as a people committed to the coming of the realm of God.

JESUS THE MAN, CHRIST THE LIBERATING NARRATIVE

Christians need to keep in mind that a large amount of the Christian Scriptures was written when orthodoxy was not a major issue. This may explain why we have differing accounts. The writers were reflecting creatively on the life of Jesus rather than trying to tie together a water-tight orthodoxy. It is strangely ironic that latter-day Christians have picked up these creative works and cast them in stone. These Christians have made them documents that judge orthodox belief instead of seeing them as reflections from within a context and a captured moment. Despite their localized and specific nature, they are no less valuable since religious reflection from different contexts adds to the global picture. It is absurd to regard them as infallible dictates from the pen of God, not least because the authors did not see them this way, living as they did in a changing world. As has already been hinted, it was taken for granted that Scripture was to be interpreted by all, and only when questions of identity crept in did a small group take it upon themselves to give definitive interpretations of Scripture. We must not forget that it was a move under pressure and thus not a liberating action.

This understanding frees believers to work more creatively with the texts within the contexts of their own lives, just as the earliest followers of Jesus would have done, adding to the story under the weight of their own contexts and interpretations. There was no fear of losing orthodoxy by adding more to the story, since faith was seen as an ongoing narrative linked with the lives of those who lived it and continued to adapt it in the retelling through their lived experience. We are less than honest when we construct one continuous and pure narrative from the accounts that were finally selected to comprise the canon of Scripture. We also become static in a changing world. Liberation theology makes a shift in the direction of the early movement by engaging with the texts in a critical way, this criticism springing as it does from lived experience.

As a Celt, I come from a powerful narrative tradition and am drawn to the notion that the transforming power of the Jesus tradition lies in the ability of the tale to adapt and expand. The Celtic peoples have been oppressed for many centuries, and through the telling of our stories, we have kept pride and identity alive under the weight of a dominant culture. Like many other dominated people, we have often had our story told for us from the viewpoint of the victors, but it was not our story at all since it did not spring from our landscape and our skins. Therefore, all it told was a false past meant to demoralize us and keep us silent and subservient. I am proud to say we were never silent. The stories were passed on, the heroes became larger than life, and the culture grew. The culture grew because its expectations were carried in the stories, and the stories remained rooted in the hopes and reality of life. Many of the original characters became far grander but were still superseded by the story itself. The hope outgrew the actors.

From this background I find it comforting to understand the early followers of Jesus as a narrative people, a people who told stories about the man of Nazareth that soon superseded his life under the weight of their oppressing circumstances. What was never lost, however, was the belief in Emmanuel, God with us. It could be argued that the Gospel writers were narrating the life of their community through the life of Jesus, in the midst of which was the Christ, the power of transformation and liberation, the energy that brings change and freedom. The Christ, it could be said, is the total narrative, not just one character within it. Jesus of Nazareth was certainly part of that powerful narrative but not the whole story. Without others and the power of praxis there would be no story, let alone a memorable one. Jesus was a powerful symbol within the story of the liberating Christ. He was the flesh and blood of Emmanuel in that he, and others, chose to live as though the power of God were fully manifest. The mistake that Christianity has made is to suggest that the narrative of the Christ begins and ends with the divine/man Jesus. Christianity has fossilized a powerful story, capturing it in one historical moment and in this way rendering it impotent. As I have already mentioned, there is a great deal of worldly power involved in controlling the story line, and the history of Christianity is not without its Master Narrators.

However, as we may expect, the history of Christianity is also littered with those who tell an alternate tale. Many of the magical-mystical storytellers were consigned to the flames or marginalized as heretics. Nevertheless, some found acceptable language with which to challenge the Grand Narrative. Much mystical and visionary material, particularly that of women, raised the possibility of alternate ways. Women often had to rely on the voice of God in order to get their own heard at all. Those such as Margery Kempe and Hildegard of Bingen,[1] although strong women, never failed to refer to themselves as poor creatures or feeble women. The references were not altogether Christian humility. Certainly, Margery was not known for her humility. It was a straightforward attempt to protect themselves from the hierarchy. Could they help it if Christ put challenging words on their lips? Indeed, they could not, being as poor and wrecked as they were. In truth what they were doing was exactly what the Gospel writers did: they took seriously the liberating power of Emmanuel, and they told it as it was in their situations. Yes, they adapted and enlarged the received stories, but they remained true to the power that overcomes oppression. They saw other ways, and they conveyed them through the person of Jesus.

Liberation theology has to an extent built on their heritage. It has called those to voice who have been silenced for generations. However, the time has now come for us to find the voices that emerge from our landscapes and claim the voices as our own. This will be as mystical and as materially historical an event as the voices of visionaries ever were. Nothing will be lost by claiming the voices as our own, and it could signal our religious maturity. We no longer rely on the disembodied God to show us but engage with Christ understood as narrative, vision, and imagination, passionately committed to creative growth and liberation. That appears to be what those who provided us with narratives were doing in the first place. They were not a people given to orthodoxy. They were committed to unfolding the narrative through praxis.

THY KINGDOM COME

Jesus and those around him engaged with scripture and the world in which they lived in order to find a sense of God's presence. Perhaps more than most people today, they would have been aware of the signs of the times as they hoped for the arrival of the kingdom of God. This kingdom had been awaited a long time and, on the one hand, could not be rushed and, on the other, was expected at any moment. In other words Jesus and his followers lived in a situation of tension between great hopes and the stark reality of everyday life. It appears from the accounts we have that they preferred to live rooted in their hopes rather than drained by apparently unchanging reality. Further, they chose to live as if those hopes were already fulfilled rather than view them as something in the future. What did they hope for and live for?

The world in which Jesus lived was brimming with eschatological expectation. The kingdom was not far off. The Messiah would be closely followed by the return of God to Mount Zion whereupon all the ills of the earth would be put right. There were many variations on the theme, as we can see from the Gospel accounts, which provide a limited sample of contemporary thought. The concept of the kingdom had undergone many transformations since its birth in the kingship ideals of Egypt and Babylon. For example, under Iranian influence, it added a transcendent feel, with the introduction of the end time, the idea of justice, and right living, which would bring about the security of the nation.

Whatever the modifications, the Jews always perceived religion as the politics of God. In many ways the politics were radicalized due to the additions. For example, the idea of transcendence gave a more cosmic understanding of evil. This did not mean that the expectations for the kingdom became any less rooted in this earth and the present time. However, by the first century C.E. a clear distinction emerged between this world, its end, and the setting in place of a new order. For many people things that were believed to be possible in this world became transposed onto another place and time that were eternal and unchanging. Therefore, along with the collapse of original Jewish hope came an unhelpful notion that things could be achieved in such a way that they could never be undone. The psychic landscape changed significantly from a circle of hope, committed action, change, and back to hope to divine intervention and unchanging absolutes. In a real sense, I wish to say that the human spirit was crushed. It is easy to see how from that point, engagement with the world became replaced by moral paralysis within it and a desire to flee from it. Instead of being empowering archetypes, the ideas of Messiah and the kingdom of God became theological and political crutches. They were spiritual excuses for nonengagement with the real stuff of life.

Jesus and his followers were based in Galilee, which was a politically volatile area. Many of the inhabitants eagerly awaited the forthcoming kingdom because they were cynical about religious rule and the legalism that accompanied it as well as being fiercely nationalistic and therefore anti-Roman. From the accounts that we have Jesus comes across as a man of his time, a political animal who opposed the elitism of the Pharisees and spoke for the inclusion of poor people in matters of religion and politics. The kingdom of God would bring with it the end of oppression in this world, not just the next.

The teaching of Jesus and his actions, for example, healing and exorcising, demonstrate the way in which the kingdom of God breaks through into the world. It is unlikely that Jesus would have suggested that the kingdom was already complete while political oppression continued. The Gospel writers give us the impression that Jesus acted as an agent of messianic hope for those who heard him. He was a Jew who clearly believed that metaphysics could not, and should not, dim hopes for embodied liberation in the here and now. He was in many ways an

agent for his own hope. After all, he went to Jerusalem not really knowing whether God would appear once more on Mount Zion. The report
of his final words haunts us and presents us with the real challenge,
which is the uncertainty. Jesus proclaimed the coming of the kingdom
and lived as though it were here but still ended up on a cross because
the world could not share the vision to the same degree.

Those whose hope for the kingdom had been as high as Jesus' had
a great deal of rethinking to do when Jesus was crucified, and unfortunately, their faith left them. Rather than live with the harsh reality that
nothing is guaranteed and the kingdom comes slowly and partially,
they eased their pain by declaring that the kingdom is here for those
with eyes to see it. In other words, they moved in the direction of saving
metaphysics. It has to be acknowledged that they did not go overboard
in that direction as the churches have subsequently done. Yet they did
declare that the Messiah rightly understood is the Suffering Servant of
Isaiah and not the political figure so long wished for. The Christ then
is transformed from One who will not rest until all oppression is overcome into the One who will suffer with you.

The various theologies of liberation have highlighted what a backward step such imaging turned out to be. This lack of faith on the part
of the early church had a number of regrettable consequences. For
example, a wedge was driven between Christians and Jews, the former
declaring that the latter's messianic hopes were misplaced. Declaring
Jesus as the Messiah has spilled over into all kinds of imperialism, as we
have seen. The Suffering Servant model of messiahship is more pliable
when it comes to political exploitation than the Messiah who would free
the oppressed. The kingdom was clearly not in the world. The early followers concluded that it was therefore not meant to be, and messianic
expectations became spiritualism under the weight of unfulfilled expectations. It would be unfair to suggest that the early writers did not show
a certain tension between wishing to declare Jesus as the Messiah and
being aware that the kingdom had yet to arrive. They wrestled with it
but still for the most part came down in favor of seeing Jesus as the final-
ization of an ideal, and in so doing they rendered him useless. When he
stands as an example between the points of tension of what may be and
what is not yet, he acts as an inspiration and hope. When he is declared
as more than that, he lulls us into a false hope and one that ensures that
the kingdom never comes on earth. We have seen how easy it is for
Christians to exploit and abuse in the name of their religion, and this is
a direct result of the notion of the once-and-for-all Messiah.

The Gospel writers always managed to hang on to the idea that the
world will need to be turned completely on its head, even when stating

that the kingdom is here. The disciples continued healing, and there is evidence from Acts that a group practiced a radical form of economics by sharing all they had and taking care of the vulnerable in their community. They kept working for it, despite declaring its presence; we have lost this knack in the community sense. One interesting notion is that those who will work for the kingdom are welcomed without having to repent first. Certainly, working in a nonhierarchical and empowering way would mean a radical change from the dominant system, but personal purity seems of little importance, compared to getting one's hands dirty in order to change the world.

Despite the Gospel writers' acknowledgment that people need to work together for change, they seem to suggest that the kingdom is a universal phenomenon that has to be everywhere or nowhere. Once again this lends itself more to metaphysics than to reality and in some way diminishes the value of the kingdom. Such divine intervention takes the initiative out of the hands of people and makes them pawns in the ultimate power-over situation. Jesus, it seems, imagined the kingdom as a place in which power-over would not be exerted. We are left wondering whether divine power, when used in such a way, is any better than secular power. Both render people powerless, and that does not sound like good news to me. The history of Christianity demonstrates how people have been abused by such a scheme.

The kingdom means at the least the full engagement of free individuals in the struggle for justice in each corner of their lives. It would appear to be a struggle that is both won and lost, but that, for me, is where the eternal relevance of Christ lies. That is, people will always have to search for radical and liberating alternatives within their lived experience and in so doing are witnessing to another way. They are heralding the kingdom and living as if God were about to appear. The most developed meditation on the theme of eschatology is in John's Gospel where the author plays with the notion that the time (kingdom) is coming but is also here. Is it really too simple to suggest that the author understood that we have the potential to change the world, but we more often than not do it only in parts and imperfectly? However, the will can be there, and this is the commitment to effort that makes some call themselves Christian. This commitment to use one's potential to overcome oppression, and not in pursuit of eternal salvation, can rightly be called working for the kingdom. The kingdom is not dispensed in a blaze of heavenly glory but is painfully drawn out from each ruptured situation and relationship only to be overshadowed again by the pressures of dominating values, to rise once more in a smile, in resistance, and in each hope-filled imaginative action. This is embodied, rising as it does from the bodies of people and their hopes for and relation with one another and the world.

THE CHRIST OF HISTORY?

Liberation theologies still wish to start with the historical Jesus rather than with philosophical notions about how to save the world. This historical figure is extremely hard to find, except in the most general way. I am not even convinced that liberation theologians look for the historical Jesus, combining as they do general statements about his life and critical engagement with the stories. They are not keen to slavishly follow each small move that Jesus made, and they are at times not slow to criticize him. For example, Latin American women have suggested that the way in which Jesus spoke to the Syro-Phoenician woman left a lot to be desired, and they accuse him of both sexism and racism during the encounter. Liberation theologians are not looking for a historical figure who will tell them what to do because they know only too well the negative side of such a figure. He is the conqueror who removes their culture and dignity in the pursuit of a kind of uniformity rooted in another time and place. He is the one who declares all they are to be inferior. This Jesus is a construction of Western values and bears little resemblance to the real Jesus of history, but the so-called historicity of the man is used as a stick with which to beat the outsiders.

Liberation theologians have no wish to engage with this figure. However, despite the fact that they point out the constructed nature of Christ, they are in danger of doing the same thing. Certainly, the Christ imaged by liberation theologians tends to be a more user-friendly model, but are they really guilty of the thing they criticize—making Christ in their own image?

The answer is that they are. How wrong is that? Liberation theologians are looking for a Christ who will alter oppressive situations, not One who will justify exploitation and global conquest. They need to image a Christ who experiences all that they do, One who lives their reality. At the same time they have no desire to impose this image on others, except perhaps those who are exploitative in their lives. This is where they differ from those who carried the conquering Christ throughout the world. The historical Jesus then takes on a rather flexible nature, being able, from a limited set of lived experiences, to speak to all people at all times.

Traditional theology would mark this transition as that between the historical Jesus and the Christ of faith. The latter is able in some degree to transcend the former, yet at the same time remains rooted in him.

This Christ of faith is also not without problems since Christ was as much to blame for the pain, suffering, and cultural and physical genocide that have been spread by Christians. This Christ may be even more to blame since Christ can be created from tradition as much as from the pages of the Book. At least a book has a certain number of pages while tradition is theoretically endless. The tradition is male, white, Western, and elitist. The Christ of faith who rises from this landscape is not altogether a liberative figure. It is not an easy matter to distinguish between the Christ of faith and the Jesus of history. The lines are blurred even in the Gospel accounts where, for example, the political preacher becomes imaged as having his genesis in virginal conception. Or the political prisoner and martyr becomes the once-and-for-all sacrifice for the forgiveness of sins.

This tendency to blur the edges gives a skewed picture, changing the story from that of transforming praxis and liberation to personal salvation. This, as I have already stated, was a backward step. Amidst all this negativity it would be a good time to acknowledge that I do understand people have been spurred on to lead extremely good and inspirational lives by both Christs in question. Nonetheless, it is my belief that these individual acts are far outweighed by the callous way in which both concepts have been used to underpin conquest and genocide.

The Christ who was born of a virgin, lived dispensing God's grace, died for the forgiveness of sins, and rose again in glory is the foundation stone for pain, suffering, and abuse of others. It is here at our mothers' knees and in the bosom of mother church that we learn flesh does not matter since it leads to sin and will have to be transformed at the resurrection. We learn that Christianity is the only truth and that people have certain hierarchical roles within it in church and family. It is here that we learn that the rest of the world is pagan, that it is divided into Christian and non-Christian. The "non-" in front of "Christian" also carries implications for the humanness, or nonhumanness, of those who fall into that category. It is here that we learn that marriage is ordained by God and that those who are nonheterosexual are also nonpersons.

It is then I hope quite obvious that when acts of emotional, economic, and physical horror emerge in Christian countries, churches, and the individual lives of Christians, far from being surprised we should to a degree have expected such acts. The Holocaust should at least have taught us this. Hitler did not invent the idea of anti-Semitism; the church had that idea for generations before him and thus numbed people to the humanness of Jews. They became a stereotype, Christ killers who deserved little sympathy. Jews/Judases were not real people at all. From a Christian European landscape the horror of the

Holocaust arose. Hitler merely took advantage of it for his own political ends.

The Christ of faith has not been the universal liberator one may have hoped for. It is possible for liberation theologians to create their own Christ of faith, who mirrors their concerns and spreads their own religious/theological culture, but would this really be a step forward? Are they right to start with the limited Jesus of history that we dimly see through the lens of time, culture, class, and gender in the pages of the Gospels? As we have seen, this allows them to be less worried about orthodoxy than they may once have been. It also puts them in touch with a rich stream of kingdom theology of which Jesus was aware. However, it also ties them to the past in a way that Daphne Hampson, among others, has shown is not always useful. By constantly referring to the time of Jesus, which is necessary if we are to view the man, we run the risk of getting caught up in the class and gender issues of his day and ignoring the signs of our times.

Hampson[2] illustrates this in relation to the long and bitter women's ordination debate. Emotions ran high on both sides, and for the most part, both sides appealed to the Jesus of history and came to opposite conclusions. In truth both read back into the life of Jesus issues more current today. What the real Jesus might have thought about the issue is beyond recovery, but how relevant is the opinion of a first-century Jew to modern Christian practice anyway? Those who opposed the ordination of women declared correctly that Jesus did not ordain women. Those who supported the ordination of women claimed falsely that Jesus treated women in a way that was unusual for his time, that he gave them greater respect than they would have received. This is incorrect in two ways: he was not always respectful, and he did not always treat them with equality. We now have evidence that women played a more public role in first-century Judaism than was once supposed. Therefore, looking to the historical Jesus could lead us to the conclusion that women should not be ordained. Tradition and the Christ of faith would support this finding. The Jesus of history might well have been a man who did not support the equality of women, even though a certain proportion of his contemporaries did so.

Should this in itself put an end to the question? For some it should, while for others such an ending would signal the nonviability of Christianity in the twentieth century and beyond. They would argue that a religion that cannot keep pace with the justice issues of the day has lost its grip on reality. The metaphysics of Christianity deals with this by speaking of being in the world but not of it; the notion is that God has a set of rules that are quite beyond human comprehension. The Jesus of history has strangely enough fallen victim to metaphysics in the same way as the Christ of faith and therefore presents us with similar problems.

We could perhaps have expected that somebody rooted in history as this notion of Jesus suggests would be less prone to manipulation through metaphysics than an altogether more ethereal Christ. However, this displays a rather naive understanding of history, which is no more than interpretation. In the West we have developed an unfortunate habit of thinking that history consists of a series of indisputable facts. This approach is related to our position in regard to the writing of history. We have written it from the point of view of the victors and do not wish to have our history challenged. It suits our purpose to believe that the way it is written is the way it was. This approach prevailed in both religious and secular history until relatively recently when we came to understand that once an event is over, it is no longer fact but falls into the realm of interpretation.

Psychologists[3] have highlighted the diversity of human interpretation. People who witness the same event and are asked to give a factual description only moments later vary enormously in their descriptions. They also have a tendency to interpret what they saw in the so-called factual description. These interpretations are directly related to the life experience of the subjects. This innate and quite natural subjectivity makes it impossible to claim any absolute certainty about an event no more than minutes old. What can be done is to gain general impressions of what may have happened from similar reports even if they are overlaid heavily with subjectivity. Reality is not always as controlled as psychological experiments. Therefore, it is far more open to interpretation when we are conveying facts than it makes us comfortable to admit. History, then, is an immediate and rainbow-colored series of interpretations.

Looking for the historical Jesus is bound to present us with a range of possibilities that can be seen either as dead ends or as creative opportunities. Carol Christ in her attempts to find a usable history for theology has developed a creative approach to history.[4] Her search is based on the need for women to find aspects of deity with which they can intimately connect, the instinct that the female represents the Divine to the same extent as the male, and anthropology and sacred stories that show, at least, a veiled Goddess. At times the veil slips, and patriarchal assumptions placed layer upon layer cannot hide her face. Carol Christ's method requires that we move beyond the overemphasis on texts that the West has come to rely on and look at physical evidence in the earth, in our bodies, and in our hearts. She suggests that there is a need to read the silences of the past and to engage imaginatively with them. First and foremost history, she declares, is the ground on which we stand.

I would like to argue that it is in fact our imaginative engagement with the ground on which we stand. What of the events that came before our time? How may we consider them? The answer, it would seem, is twofold: as the interpretations by others of their own history and as our cultural memories.

As we see, the Jesus of history and the Christ of faith present certain problems. What needs to be overcome is a rooting in the limited facts of history that can lead to paralysis or a construction of Christ that leads to exploitation and abuse. Another angle seems necessary. Therefore, I wish to suggest the Christ of history, which I understand to have grown out of the resurrection. The Gospel stories show that those who were part of the life of Jesus and engaged with the struggle for alternative realities had their memories jogged and their grief put to good use by familiar action, that of breaking bread. Who knows who actually broke that postcrucifixion bread? It is really not important. What is significant is that it awoke a powerful, painful memory that spurred people on. It made them declare that the Messiah was risen, through the living and sharing of their lives, and was gone before them to Galilee, a place of political dissent. So what was awakened in the friends of the man Jesus? It is my contention that the passion of his political engagement once more came to light in the stunned and disappointed men, kindled by the power of familiar action and memory. The ground on which they stood became charged with potential for change, and they were gripped with the passion to effect it.

The Christ of history is not a figure whose life can be plotted from birth to death with pinpoint accuracy and whose words are cast in stone. Christ's history is far more exciting and creative than that. Christ is not a set of facts but a powerful memory coupled with liberative action. This is not to claim unique status for Christ since many people provide powerful memories for others on a personal and community basis. It is more than unfortunate that the combination of imperial power and Greek metaphysics crushed the memory of a small, dynamic movement and reinvented it as a colonial conqueror.

The Christ of history provides us with a family story of passion and resistance rather than a set of laid-out rules and regulations. Our relationship with Christ can be imaginative and creative as we carry forward this family narrative into future generations. Mary Daly and others believe that we have to abandon this narrative altogether to the scrap heap of patriarchy. Christianity is beyond hope. This view can gain a great deal of sympathy but is rather naive. Can we really walk away from our history and culture? Can we just blank out our memory? We are not rootless people, and to attempt to be so is a project that must fail. Rather than run from the tyranny of some of our past memories, we would do better to face them and move on. Doing this involves pain, intense listening, space, and the honesty by which we are willing for all to be heard. The time of hiding difficult stories under the blanket of conformity has to be over if our future is to hold within it powerful narrative memories of our present. The old Jesus of history made it necessary for the world to wait in expectation until everyone told the same story, but the re-imaged Christ of history allows for each one to weave and share his or her own narrative.

We would be unwise to walk away as Daly suggests because these stories that we tell are rooted in our culture, and even in the most secular environment there remain traces of our religious heritage. To attempt to ignore this would in a sense be to lose contact with the things that may still harm us. It seems like deliberately throwing oneself into the darkness when what is really needed is to change the lighting. The shadows that are cast come from the powerful symbols and images of the Divine that reside at the center of our culture.

How do we re-image through the Christ of history in such a way that the destructive tendencies are purged from our belief system and our way of life? The first task is perhaps to address underlying metaphysics because as we have seen time and again, such dualism leads to abuses of both people and the planet. It has always puzzled me that the interpretations that we have, the Gospels, speak of the outpouring of God into flesh, yet the faith still operates on dualistic metaphysics. Surely, we have a memory that tells us that there never was a division between Creator and created? Therefore, rather than divide the world into dualisms that in reality can also be interpreted as the good and the not-so-good, for example, spirit/flesh, man/woman, reason/intuition, and culture/nature, we should embrace the whole. We should not abandon the expectations that we place on the higher aspects; rather, we should expect them on this earth and in our lives.

The memory that we have appears to show that divine and human coexist in the created order and that acknowledging this leads to creative interactions and transformations of both. Metaphysics are not overcome in this rational and scientific world of ours. I am arguing for a squeezing together of expectations, that is, what we hope the realm of metaphysics can achieve we should believe the created order can make real. Divine intervention then occurs whenever we act. This bold statement assumes that these actions have a certain quality. However, far from being of the ethereal and pure type, they of necessity will be messy because they occur in the real world where the privilege of tidy absolutes does not apply.

Divine intervention does not guarantee that all will be well. It never has. It means that a struggle is going on, a striving for liberation from the dysfunctional and destructive tendencies in the world. The Christ of history is the creative explosion of countercultural alternatives brought about by communities of people who act as though the kingdom were already here, people who live the hopes of metaphysics in their everyday lives.

The Christ of history is partial, messy, and never absolute. Further, this Christ can never escape the realities of this world since liberative history is beneath our feet and is grasped or is gone.

THE FLESH BECOMES WORD

The Jesus of memory and interpretation was portrayed as an earthy man sharing touch, engaging with nature, making strong political statements through the symbolic use of food (both during the Last Supper and in the feedings of thousands Jesus enacted shared power and the interconnected nature of flourishing; when each gives and receives, there is more than enough, and all are empowered through the equality of give-and-take; the actions that are now eucharistic are also powerful political symbols since all receive equally in cultures where inequality of access to food and wealth is blatantly obvious), and using fluid from his body to heal. As we have seen, his understanding of the part he and others could play in creating the kingdom relied more on hard work and physical involvement with people than on metaphysical intervention. So what can we do with this memory in order to embody the Christ of history?

The answer in part seems to be rooting deep, grounding in our world and our selves, and bursting forth from the passion we find within. Carter Heyward has developed the idea of *dunamis* and erotic connection,[5] and this seems to be one way ahead. One way in which the Christ of history explodes into the reality of everyday life in an intimate and transforming way is through something as simple and as powerfully frightening as touch. The power of touch, as witnessed in the life of Jesus and others, has been forgotten. Perhaps because the church fathers could focus only on the negative power of touch and so laid such strong prohibitions against it, we have forgotten how to do it. The Christ of history though, no longer being that of historical facts, becomes the Christ of magical-mystical engagement rooted in the unfolding history of intimacy and empowerment. This Christ is the One who knew the power of touch to heal or to destroy and understood that the kingdom rests on the way in which we choose to touch one another and the world.

The Christ of history enables the flesh to become word and is not the Word made flesh. The colonization of Sophia (Wisdom) into Logos (Word) by the Christian tradition was a regrettable step. Not only did it deny the Divine a female face, but it also made heady a reality that was embodied. Divine Wisdom as understood in the Hebrew Scriptures was active among the people, walking in the marketplace and connecting people with the earth and everyday concerns.[6] She was understood as the Divine who led people to wisdom through rooting and grounding in themselves and their cultures. The women and men who followed her were often accused of being sexually immoral because of their sensual connection with creation in the pursuit of wisdom. However, this is best understood as exaggeration on the part of those who would prefer a more rigid and hierarchical system of belief, the priestly caste. Unfortunately for them, those who find their truth through embodiment cannot be easily controlled. The wisdom that we gain through our bodies goes far deeper and convinces us to a greater extent than that found in our heads alone.

By placing experience as the starting point of theological reflection, liberation theology moves us back to our bodies. We can see how that understanding has become developed as the various theologies of liberation take root. Feminist, gay, and lesbian theologies perhaps are the most concerned with what has become known as body theology.[7] The body, far from being seen as sinful flesh and the site of all evil, has emerged as a place of revelation and moral imperatives. The broken, bleeding, and oppressed bodies of people demand that reality is to be changed and that they are to be made whole again—in this world. In this way the flesh is speaking and being heard as a site of positive theological significance. It is also asserted that we are our bodies. There is no other part of us that is more who we truly are, such as the soul, as once was argued.

This notion, if it is to be understood as Christian, requires a shift in traditional teaching. It is a shift that is made possible through process theology where we come to see the world progressing and striving for fulfillment rather than decaying. It is an easy shift if we understand the notion of incarnation against its Jewish, and particularly wisdom, background rather than through the inculturation of Greek philosophy. A God who walks with the people and is involved in the messy business of life, not just the purified religious aspects, will burst through in outrageous creativity in the lives of people and the fabric of the universe, particularly when the existence of both is being diminished through exploitation. This God will not descend from another realm like the gods of the Greek pantheon. The universe, both human and otherwise, flourishes when given space and freedom, and it is in the divine nature of both to push for this reality. The God who bursts forth is not a metaphysical being who is removed from the fabric of creation but the divine creativity inherent in each atom and fiber. This Emmanuel (God with us) is closer to us than we are to ourselves, as the mystics say, because it is the stuff of our embodiment. The divine thread knits the whole of creation together in interconnection and equality. The Christ, I would like to suggest, is the creative bursting forth of shared divinity in specific manifestations according to desire. This Christ explodes in embodied empowerment in history and demands alternatives.

Nothing of consequence would be said if this explosive Christ simply appeared as a separate entity and consoled downtrodden people. The embodied power in all creation makes the Christ a transforming reality. The flesh made word enables us to find a voice and to make our desires known. There are any number of examples of how this vision transforms the landscape of our lives: those who are starving present themselves as moral imperatives for the rest of us, those who are poisoned by toxic waste challenge the ethics of business and profit, while those who labor under the genocidal reality of advanced capitalism present their bodies as a moral challenge to the Christian world. When the flesh is word, there can be no talk of reward in heaven. The bodies of these people are their heaven or hell; they will not wait and be soothed by pious utterances. The flesh enables Sophia (Wisdom) to find creative alternatives.

The flesh as word also demands that absolutes are to be placed to one side and listening is to take the place of unilateral dictation. Reality is constantly changing, and what is required is the liberation of empowered speech and hearing, not the misplaced confidence of eternal answers. The flesh has been silenced by metaphysics, hierarchy, and once-and-for-all incarnation. The narrative Christ speaks but not just from the head, through the whole body, and this voice returns power to people. The tower of Babel is an interesting example of how understanding is impaired by hierarchy. We do not hear so well at a distance, particularly when that distance is up. The narrative Christ of history, who is at the center of creation, translates the babble through engaging us in commitment to one another. This Christ illuminates the landscape through the power of intimate connection. The fact that we hear and see does not guarantee that we will achieve the required outcome, but it does commit us to the struggle. By taking the flesh seriously, we open up a whole new landscape that has previously been veiled in distrust and original sin. We open ourselves to the transforming power of incarnation.

THE POWER OF CHRIST

How are we to understand the power of Christ? It is no longer possible to say that the power of Christ lies in the heavens and intervenes to make all things well at the end of time, if not now. The whole question of power has been a vexed one for liberation theology, and it becomes no less so when considering Christology. The patriarchal imposition of power-over has caused suffering throughout the world, and liberation theologians first reflected upon this application of power. However, they were slower to consider how the power within systems of religion adversely affected people and possibly even slower to admit that the same power structures were in place in secular and religious systems.

The power of the enfleshed, narrative Christ lies in intimate connection and in the power that Heyward and others have called erotic. This raw, dynamic energy that exists within and between us is the power of Christ, the power that can burst out and transform. We have to understand ourselves as fully enfleshed if this power is to find its full expression. The impotency of metaphysics is always a danger in Christian theology. It seems entirely possible that what the early Christian writers were conveying about incarnation was not a once-and-for-all event but the knowledge that unless we are fully in our bodies, we will never be able to fully explore our divinity.

Even the early fathers, as influenced as they were by Greek dualism, understood that Jesus was most fully divine when he was most fully human. This meant not that he left the world but that he entered more fully into it. The fathers also suggested that Christ became man so that all may become divine.[8] I would like to change their emphasis but accept their vision. It was not the incarnation of the only Child of God that allowed believers to achieve union with the Divine, usually after death, but the bursting forth of the Divine that makes it possible for all to grasp the same power. I would go along more with Joan Casanas who says, "Anyone who makes an opening as he did wants others to enlarge it."[9] We remember Jesus because he is part of our cultural heritage, but others made an equally large gap in the veil between disempowerment and divine creativity. The task for us all is to bring the power of Christ to the forefront, to make empowered living the reality for all.

Perhaps when we grasp the power of erotic connection between us, we will have collapsed the final barrier to empowerment that dualism sets in place, the uniqueness of Christ. Viewing Christ as unique renders us powerless and is, in truth, as oppressive as any other patriarchal hierarchy. That has been the subject of this book. However, when Christ is seen as the power released through intimate and erotic connection, all such potential for exploitation is overcome. Christ becomes the dynamism between people and the earth rather than a white, celibate male who judges according to the particular incarnation of Jesus of Nazareth.

For many Christians, the power of Christ is seen to lie in the resurrection—without which they would argue there is no Christianity. Once again there is a danger in announcing the resurrection as an event solely connected with the man Jesus. As I have already said, I see the Christ of history as springing from the resurrection, but I do not wish to imply the raising of a particular body. Christianity is bigger than this. Those who witnessed the resurrection experienced the memory of the man and the power of the Christ of history, that is, the power to resist embedded in passionate and intimate connection. These accounts are later additions to the Gospels and can be seen in two ways, either as last-minute attempts to add weight to the argument or as reflections upon the power of Christ (as I am now defining it). If we take the latter view, we see that groups of crushed and frightened individuals found, through shared memory and the weight of their circumstances, that the historical Christ is available in all times and places. This power is not lost with the person. Is it too outrageous to suggest that the story of the Transfiguration signaled the acceptance of the departure of the man Jesus but the embrace of the power of Christ, which remains constant? Is that what the tongues of fire really symbolized, the passion and empowerment of incarnation? Do we too need to experience a transfiguration, a letting go of the man, just as we are told Mary Magdalene was commanded to do, and a full embrace of the fiery power that lies in every fiber of our beings?

This is no easy matter since we have been told religious tales that make us afraid of power, particularly embodied power. Eve is set before us as an example of how afraid we should really be since she interacted with the world in a truly sensual and embodied way, taking joy as she did in the beauty of creation. The result was expulsion from paradise. Christian theology has viewed this as the tragedy that required the death of the Child of God to atone for it, while Jewish theology views it as one step toward the fulfillment of creation. I wish to side with the Jewish interpretation to make the point that paradise is not an ideal state to be in; it is unreal. As Mary Daly has pointed out, it is a walled-in, confined space where freedom is limited. This is not an attractive prospect and is certainly not the sort of fulfillment of the power of God/Christ that I would hope for. Can we instead see Eve as the fore-mother of another tradition that encouraged engagement with the real stuff of life in order to enjoy its beauty, experience its power, and risk its dangers? Elisabeth Schüssler Fiorenza has shown us that another tradition does exist in the Hebrew canon, and that is the Sophia tradition in which she places Jesus. It is a tradition in which power is shared and in this way increased. How ironic that Jesus, who shared the power of embodied wisdom with those around him, has since been imaged as the sole power holder, the One who alone has saved the whole world.

Such an approach, through placing power among and within people, is accused of making redundant any notion of the transcendence of God/Christ. However, this is not entirely true if we are able to think in terms of radical immanence rather than transcendence, which gives the impression of moving away. The radically immanent Christ is the One who increases in the sharing and therefore to some degree does transcend individual parts of the praxis. Through the power of intimate connection, individuals are carried beyond their own limitations into a greater whole, yet they remain embodied and connected with themselves and with one another. The connection makes the expansion real and possible.

I do not wish to limit this to human beings since connection with the earth is equally powerful because it too carries the dynamic power of creativity. It seems that Christianity as an incarnational religion has placed the emphasis on transcendence too strongly, which has resulted in a rather halfhearted engagement with the world by many Christians. It has also meant that promises of salvation have been viewed as more absolute. Where would we find ourselves if we understood the crucifixion as a statement about the death of transcendence? After all, a truly transcendent God could avoid such a fate and the placing of the kingdom in the hands of humanity—but a humanity that understands itself as divine by birth.

A CHRISTOLOGY OF RISK

Moving as I wish to do from the once-and-for-all Child of God to a more free-flowing Christ is risky business because this notion implies that Christ is only a possibility and not a guarantee. We place at risk salvation, but I think we also make the coming of the kingdom a more urgent requirement and more possible. In other words I am willing to sacrifice salvation for liberation and the kingdom. I am taking salvation to have the more personalized meaning that it has had over the centuries and has today in evangelical quarters. This personal relationship with the Savior of the world, leading to individual salvation, is one that I wish to question in pursuit of a liberative Christology.

I believe a Christology of risk is perfectly in line with a religion that has incarnation at the heart. Becoming flesh is risky because it leaves behind all the certainty of metaphysical absolutes. The stories of the creation of the world and of the crucifixion of Jesus highlight the point—nothing is guaranteed once we commit to life. (The crucifixion cannot be seen as salvific if this line of thought is to hold.) The freedom required for the diverse wonder of creation to manifest is a huge risk. The God that Christians proclaim did take that risk in creation and in incarnation since the stories maintain a degree of free will on the creative order of Jesus, thus keeping the redemptive tension. From a traditional point of view, we can say that God took the risk of redeeming a world that did not want it with a Child who had the ability to run away. God took the risk of leaping into flesh, yet we have been encouraged to resist our enfleshment.

A Christology of risk means that the kingdom is always somewhere between the gloriously successful empowerment of ourselves and others, the devastatingly wrong and the mundanely unimaginative. Imagination is a key point in our risk taking. If we are to break out of the hold that oppressive systems increasingly seem to have on the world, then vision empowered by imagination is crucial. We have to live as though the kingdom were already here, live counterculturally, live transgressively. We have to incarnate the transgressive Christ, the One who plays with existing categories and breaks boundaries. The aim is a freer and more creative space for all in which aspects of incarnation not yet thought of can take root. By limiting our Christology to Jesus, we are in danger of reliving his limitations and prejudices. As we have seen, he appeared to have some that were embedded in his world. The woman with the hemorrhage is just one example illustrating that Jesus may have allowed his own power of connection to be limited by his cultural surroundings and he had to be carried forward to break boundaries by the touch of another. The erotic, transgressive Christ spurs us on to be limitless and without boundary. We are to face imaginatively those erected in our own minds, cultures, religious systems, and environments and overcome them through the power of intimate connection.

This argument is not for an evolutionary view of Christ as we find in Teilhard de Chardin with his concept of the Omega Point. Although this idea allows for movement, it fails to take the ultimate step in the direction of risk by saying there is no fixed end point; what we face is an open future, spreading as it does into eternity. We are as truly in the process as God is; therefore, all we can do is really be embodied in it rather than attempt to be passive observers. We are cocreators and (or not) coredeemers with the Christ. Through our actions, we make or break people and the universe. We are in a real sense walking by faith in a resurrection hope. We cannot be sure of our Christic power triumphing in the end, but we are committed to transgressive rebellion, which will change everyday life for us and others. This process can never be declared finished and appears in any given moment to be fragile and partial.

The whole of creation is involved in this process of Christic becoming, and so no human hierarchy can be set in place. We are also challenged to a new and dynamic view of our coredeemer, nature, one that bends previously held systems. There is much hope that the Gaia[10] theory will bring us new and exciting insights into the interconnected reality of the entire universe. Perhaps we will see with scientific eyes the epiphanic, organic Christ that Kwok Pui-Lan puts forward. The Christ who erupts in many guises and often in the fabric of creation. The risky Christ, the Christ that does not have to be, yet time and again is.

LIBERATING CHRIST

Liberation theologies have exposed the connection between a hierarchical and absolute Christ and the oppressions that fill the world. In some cases this Christ has been the cause of the pain and in others merely a solid ally for existing systems of injustice. They have also found in Christ an advocate who can lift people from situations of helplessness to liberation. This is certainly true, yet a doubt still lingers in my mind, and I am concerned that power resting solely in Christ can easily be turned against people, however liberative it appears in the present. That is why I have suggested a different view of Christ—one that I hope overcomes some of the problems connected with metaphysics and Platonic Ideal Forms that have become our Christian heritage. I do not wish to diminish the memory of the man Jesus simply to say that he was part of the story and not the whole and final episode. We can learn important lessons from the accounts we have of how he appeared to affect people, but seeing him in isolation reduces the story and the power of Christ. Indeed, it transforms the real power of the Christ into oppressive regimes and fossilized doctrines.

Christ the liberator must find liberation because he has only liberated into existing categories, in other words, into the world as it is, not the world where the kingdom is thought to have arrived. For example, if the poor become well off but the system of economics is not in any way changed, there is no real emergence of the Christ and the kingdom. All that has taken place is shifting of the power base. If gay and lesbian people are able to marry, has the oppressive ideology underlying Christian marriage really been challenged? The transgressive Christ urges us to find other ways of being in the world while the Christ of history both poses the problems and provides the stage for working out the partial answers.

Liberation Christologies have brought us a long way in a short time, and it is good to reflect on where we are at the end of the millennium. But where do we go now? It is my contention that the issue of power/empowerment will be the greatest challenge of the next hundred years. We have learned for so long that the power lies elsewhere; thus, it will be a hard task to recover the divine dignity, passion, and power that are ours by birth. I suggest that by exploring the Christ of history, the enfleshed Christ who acts transgressively and takes risks, who lives in and around us, we will come closer to the kingdom than we are as the millennium closes. It is the kingdom of Jewish hope, political, just, and empowering. We must find the courage to abandon Greek metaphysics and imperial power and instead embrace the power within the whole of the created order. The Christ who is beneath our feet, before our eyes, in our hearts, and throbbing between us is able, and willing, to burst out. Seize your moment—enflesh the Christ you profess to believe in.

NOTES

1. Liberating Landscapes

1. Albert Schweitzer, *The Quest for the Historical Jesus: A Critical Study of Its Progress from Reimarus to Wrede* (New York: Macmillan, 1906).

2. We have fragments of eighty or more documents from this early period, though complete manuscripts number far fewer. New Testament scholars do acknowledge, however, that our Christological material extends well beyond the four canonical Gospels.

3. John MacQuarrie, *Jesus Christ in Modern Thought* (London: SCM, 1990).

4. W. H. C. Frend, *The Early Church* (London: Hodder, 1973).

5. Henry Chadwick, *The Early Church* (London: Pelican, 1974).

6. Rosemary Radford Ruether, *Sexism and God-Talk* (London: SCM, 1986).

7. William Harbury, *Jewish Messianism and the Cult of Christ* (London: SCM, 1998).

8. Burton L. Mack, *The Lost Gospel, the Book of Q, and Christian Origins* (Dorset, Eng.: Element, 1993). John Dominic Crossan, *The Historical Jesus: The Life of a Mediterranean Jewish Peasant* (San Francisco: Harper, 1992).

9. Gustavo Gutiérrez, *A Theology of Liberation* (London: SCM, 1974), 29.

10. Theo Witvliet, *A Place in the Sun* (New York: Orbis, 1985), 123.

11. Ibid., 124.

12. Quoted in Lisa Isherwood and Dorothea McEwan, *Introducing Feminist Theology* (Sheffield, Eng.: Sheffield Academic Press, 1993), 42.

13. Ibid., 130.

14. Rosino Gibellini, *The Liberation Theology Debate* (London: SCM, 1987), 45.

15. Witvliet, *A Place in the Sun*, 139.

16. Ibid., 141.

17. Douglas John Hall and Rosemary Ruether, *God and the Nations* (Minneapolis: Fortress Press, 1995), 97.

18. Ibid., 98.

19. Witvliet, *A Place in the Sun*, 90.

20. Vandana Shiva, quoted in Rosemary Ruether, *Women Healing Earth* (London: SCM, 1996), 67.

21. Hall and Ruether, *God and the Nations*, 99.

22. Shiva, quoted in *Women Healing Earth*, 67.

23. Hall and Ruether, *God and the Nations*, 100.

24. Ibid., 101.

25. Ibid., 102.

26. Ibid., 103.

27. Audre Lorde, *Sister Outsider: Essays and Speeches* (Trumansburg, N.Y.: Crossing Press, 1984).

28. Quoted in Marie Giblin et al., eds., *Liberation Theology: An Introductory Reader* (New York: Orbis, 1992), 82.

29. Nelle Morton, *The Journey Is Home* (Boston: Beacon, 1985).

2. Black, African, and Womanist Christologies

1. Witvliet, *A Place in the Sun*, 42.

2. Quoted in ibid., 49.

3. Ibid., 57.

4. Ibid., 60.

5. Kelly Brown Douglas, *The Black Christ* (New York: Orbis, 1994), 31.

6. Ibid., 32.

7. Ibid., 50.

8. Ibid., 62.

9. James Cone, "Jesus Christ in Black Theology," in *Liberation Theology: A Reader*, ed. Curt Coderette et al. (New York: Orbis, 1992).

10. Ibid., 147.

11. Ibid.

12. Ibid., 149.

13. Ibid., 151.

14. Ibid., 153.

15. Douglas, *The Black Christ*, 105.

16. Ibid., 107.

17. Ibid., 105.

18. Ibid., 108.

19. Ibid.

20. See the work of Delores Williams and Jacquelyn Grant (including books cited in notes 23 and 24 below).

21. Douglas, *The Black Christ*, 114.

22. Alice Walker, *Possessing the Secret of Joy* (New York: Harcourt Brace Jovanovich, 1993), 274.

23. Delores Williams, *Sisters in the Wilderness: The Challenge of Womanist God-Talk* (New York: Orbis, 1993), 169.

24. Jacquelyn Grant, *White Women's Christ, Black Woman's Jesus* (Atlanta: Scholars Press, 1989), 201.

25. Ibid., 210.

26. Ibid., 215.

27. Ibid., 220.

28. Edward Kamau Braithwaite, *Folk Culture of the Slaves in Jamaica* (London: Beacon Books, 1970), 6.

29. See John Mbiti, *African Religions and Philosophy* (New York: Anchor Books, 1970).

30. Robert Beckford, *Jesus Is Dread: Black Theology and Black Culture in Britain* (London: DLT, 1998), 17.

31. Ibid., 63.

32. Ibid., 69.

33. Ibid., 73.

34. Ibid., 74.

35. I am a founding member of the Britain and Ireland School of Feminist Theology. Despite our many attempts to network with black women's groups, we have met with little success. The issue does not appear to be racial; we are too radical for church women and too religious for secular women. We continue to keep lines of communication open.

36. Witvliet, *A Place in the Sun*, 92.

37. Ibid., 99.

38. Allan Boesak, *Black Theology: Black Power* (London: Mowbray, 1976), 11.

39. Ibid., 50.

40. Ibid., 57.

41. Ibid., 82–83.

42. Ibid., 91.

43. Witvliet, *A Place in the Sun*, 82.

44. Teresa Hinga, "Jesus Christ and the Liberation of Women in Africa," in *Feminist Theology from the Third World*, ed. Ursula King (London: SPCK, 1994), 266.

45. Ibid., 267.

46. Anne Nasimiyu-Wasike, "An African Woman's Experience," in *Liberation Theology*, 101.

47. Therese Souga, "The Christ Event from the Viewpoint of African Women," in *With Passion and Compassion*, ed. Virginia Fabella and Mercy Amba Oduyoye (New York: Orbis, 1994), 25.

48. Ibid., 22.

3. Jesus Christ Liberator?

1. Jon Sobrino, *Christology at the Crossroads* (London: SCM, 1978), 4.

2. Rudolf Bultmann, quoted in Carter Heyward, *The Redemption of God: A Theology of Mutual Relation* (Lanham, Md.: University Press of America, 1982), 28.

3. Sobrino, *Christology at the Crossroads*, 5.

4. Heyward, *The Redemption of God*, 32.

5. Ibid., 4.

6. Sobrino, *Christology at the Crossroads*, 6.

7. Ibid., 8.

8. Ibid.

9. Ibid., 10.

10. Kasper, quoted in *Christology at the Crossroads*, 10.

11. Leonardo Boff, *Jesus Christ Liberator: A Critical Christology for Our Time* (London: SPCK, 1980), 21.

12. Ibid.

13. Pannenberg, quoted in *Christology at the Crossroads*, 26.

14. Sobrino, *Christology at the Crossroads*, 194.

15. Gutiérrez, *A Theology of Liberation*, 115.

16. Ibid., 167.

17. Jon Sobrino, "Jesus and the Kingdom of God," in *Liberation Theology*, 107.

18. Ibid., 113.

19. Quoted in Boff, *Jesus Christ Liberator*, 76.

20. Ibid., 259.

21. Ibid., 207.

22. Ibid., 212.

23. Sobrino, *Christology at the Crossroads*, 180.

24. Ibid., 195.

25. Ibid., 196.

26. Ibid., 197.

27. Ibid., 202.

28. Ibid., 189.

29. Käsemann, quoted in ibid., 206.

30. Ibid., 217.

31. Boff, *Jesus Christ Liberator*, 28.

32. Rosemary Ruether, "Rift between Gutiérrez and Peru Women," *National Catholic Reporter*, October 18, 1996, 128.

33. Ibid.

34. Raquel Rodriguez, "Open Our Eyes," in *Feminist Theology from the Third World*, 220–29.

35. See Ivone Gebara in Elina Vuola, *Limits of Liberation* (Helsinki: Finnish Academy of Science and Letters, 1997).

36. Maria Clara Bingemer, "Women in the Future of the Theology of Liberation," in *Feminist Theology from the Third World*, 308–18.

37. Ibid., 317.

38. Ibid.

39. Marcella Althaus-Reed, "The Indecency of Her Teaching: Notes for a CUCEB Teaching of Feminist Theology in Europe," in *Feminist Theology in Different Contexts*, ed. Elisabeth Schüssler Fiorenza and Shawn Copeland (London: SCM, 1996), 136.

40. Elsa Tamez, "Quetzalcoatl y El Dios Cristiano," in *Cuadernos de Teologia y Cultura*, no. 6 (1992), San José, Costa Rica.

41. Nelly Ritchie, "Women and Christology," in *Through Her Eyes: Women's Theology from Latin America*, ed. Elsa Tamez (New York: Orbis, 1989), 82.

42. Ibid., 88.

43. María Pilar Aquino, "Directions and Foundations of Hispanic/Latino Theology: Toward a Mestiza Theology of Liberation," in *Mestizo Christianity: Theology from a Latino Perspective*, ed. Arturo J. Banuelas (New York: Orbis, 1995), 192–208.

44. Ivone Gebara, "A Cry for Life from Latin America," in *Spirituality of the Third World: A Cry for Life*, ed. K. C. Abraham and Bernadette Mbuy-Beya (New York: Orbis, 1994), 109–18.

45. Joan Casanas, "The Task of Making God Exist," in *The Idols of Death and the God of Life: A Theology*, ed. Pablo Richard (New York: Orbis, 1983), 139.

4. Redeemer or Redeemed?

1. Ruether, *Sexism and God-Talk*, 16.

2. Mary Daly, quoted in Mary Grey, *Redeeming the Dream* (London: SPCK, 1989), 56.

3. Mary Daly, *Beyond God the Father* (London: Women's Press, 1986), 19.

4. Ibid., 71.

5. Elisabeth Schüssler Fiorenza, quoted in Ursula King, *Women and Spirituality* (London: Macmillan, 1989), 160.

6. Mary Daly, "After the Death of God," in *Womanspirit Rising*, ed. Carol Christ and Judith Plaskow (New York: Harper and Row, 1979), 53.

7. Elisabeth Moltmann-Wendel, *A Land Flowing with Milk and Honey* (London: SCM, 1986), 63.

8. Daly, *Beyond God the Father*, 63.

9. Rosemary Ruether, "Motherearth and the Megamachine: A Theology of Liberation in a Feminine, Somatic, and Ecological Perspective," in *Womanspirit Rising*, 44.

10. Ruether, *Sexism and God-Talk*, 69.

11. Ibid., 3.

12. Ibid., 11.

13. Ibid., 28.

14. Letty Russell, *Human Liberation from a Feminist Perspective: A Theology* (Philadelphia: Westminster Press, 1974), 73.

15. Ibid., 103.

16. Ruether, *Sexism and God-Talk*, 120.

17. Ibid., 122.

18. Rosemary Ruether, *To Change the World: Christology and Cultural Criticism* (New York: Crossroad, 1988), 18.

19. Moltmann-Wendel, *A Land Flowing with Milk and Honey*, 125.

20. Ibid., 134.

21. Ibid., 172.

22. Ibid., 183.

23. Grey, *Redeeming the Dream*, 87.

24. Ibid.

25. Ibid.

26. Sharon Welch, *Communities of Resistance and Solidarity* (New York: Orbis, 1985), 89.

27. Grey, *Redeeming the Dream*, 88.

28. Ibid., 96.

29. Ibid., 97.

30. Ibid.

31. Ibid., 105.

32. Ibid., 108.

33. Rita Brock, *Journeys by Heart: A Christology of Erotic Power* (New York: Crossroad, 1988), 17.

34. Ibid., 40.

35. Ibid., 57.

36. Ibid., 66.

37. Ibid., 67.

38. Ibid., 76.

39. Ibid., 82.

40. Ibid., 98.

41. Elisabeth Schüssler Fiorenza, *Jesus: Miriam's Son, Sophia's Prophet* (New York: Continuum, 1994), 8.

42. Ibid., 14.

43. Ibid., 30.

44. Elizabeth Johnson, "Redeeming the Name of Christ," in *Freeing Theology: The Essentials of Theology in Feminist Perspective*, ed. Catherine Mowry LaCugna (New York: Harper, 1993), 122.

45. Ibid., 124.

5. Queering Christ

1. See Bernadette Brooten, *Love Between Women: Early Christian Responses to Female Homoeroticism* (Chicago: University of Chicago Press, 1996).

2. Robert Goss, *Jesus Acted Up: A Gay and Lesbian Manifesto* (New York: Harper and Row, 1993), 64.

3. Ibid., 68.

4. Heyward, *The Redemption of God*, xix.

5. Carter Heyward, *Our Passion for Justice* (New York: The Pilgrim Press, 1984), 11.

6. Ibid., 12.

7. Carter Heyward, *Touching Our Strength: The Erotic as Power and the Love of God* (New York: HarperCollins, 1989), 2.

8. Virginia Mollenkott, *Sensuous Spirituality: Out from Fundamentalism* (New York: Crossroad, 1993), 16.

9. Heyward, *Our Passion for Justice*, 18.

10. Ibid., 1.

11. Ibid., 49–50.

12. Heyward, *The Redemption of God*, 7.

13. Ibid., 3.

14. Ibid., 5.

15. Ibid., 10–11.

16. Ibid., 16.

17. Ibid., 31.

18. Ibid., 33.

19. Ibid., 37.

20. Ibid., 38.

21. Ibid., 47.

22. Ibid., 48.

23. Ibid., 53.

24. Ibid., 58.

25. Ibid., 59.

26. Michael Clark, *A Place to Start: Toward an Unapologetic Gay Liberation Theology* (Dallas: Monument Press, 1989), 105.

27. Heyward, *The Redemption of God*, 154.

28. Phyllis Graham, *The Jesus Hoax* (London: Frewin Publications, 1974), 179–80.

29. Heyward, *The Redemption of God*, 163.

30. Ibid., 164.

31. Ibid., 201.

32. Monika Hellwig, *Theology as Fine Art* (Wilmington, Del.: Michael Glazier, 1983), 10.

33. Robert Williams, quoted in Goss, *Jesus Acted Up*, 95.

34. Tom Driver, quoted in Goss, *Jesus Acted Up*, 127.

35. Robert Williams, quoted in Goss, *Jesus Acted Up*, 130.

36. See Gary Comstock, *Gay Theology Without Apology* (Cleveland: The Pilgrim Press, 1993).

37. William Countryman, *Dirt, Greed, and Sex: Sexual Ethics in the New Testament* (London: SCM, 1989).

38. Susan Faludi, *Backlash* (London: Chatto and Windus, 1992), 53.

39. See the work of Marx on the relationship between family and capital.

40. See Mary Hunt, *Fierce Tenderness* (New York: Crossroad, 1991), and Elisabeth Stuart, *Just Good Friends* (London: Mowbray, 1995).

41. Martin Stringer, "Expanding the Boundaries of Sex: An Exploration of Sexual Ethics After the Second Sexual Revolution," in *Theology and Sexuality* (Sheffield, Eng.: Sheffield Academic Press, 1997).

42. Ibid., 35.

43. Ibid., 41.

44. For work on body theology see Lisa Isherwood and Elisabeth Stuart, *Introducing Body Theology* (Sheffield, Eng.: Sheffield Academic Press, 1998).

6. Christ among the Shamans

1. Kwok Pui-Lan, "The Future of Feminist Theology: An Asian Perspective," in *Feminist Theology from the Third World*, 69.

2. See Chung Hyun Kyung, "*Han-pu-ri*: Doing Theology from a Korean Perspective," in *We Dare to Dream: Doing Theology as Asian Women*, ed. Virginia Fabella and Sun Ai Lee Park (Hong Kong: AWCCT, 1989).

3. Ibid.

4. See Ahn Sang Nim, "Feminist Theology in the Korean Church," in *We Dare to Dream*.

5. Sung-Hee Lee-Linke, "The Revival of Theology in Asia as a Product of Feminist Theology," in *Culture, Women, and Theology*, ed. John S. Pobee (Delhi: ISPCK, 1994), 76.

6. Chung Hyun Kyung, *Struggle to Be the Sun Again* (London: SCM, 1990), 54.

7. Ibid., 59.

8. Lee Oo Chung, "Korean Culture and Feminist Theology," *In God's Image* (September 1987): 37. (Published in Seoul.)

9. Ibid., 38.

10. Chung Hyun Kyung, *Struggle to Be the Sun Again*, 65.

11. Quoted in ibid., 65.

12. Ibid., 66.

13. Naomi F. Southard, "Recovery and Rediscovered Images: Spiritual Resources for Asian American Women," in *Feminist Theology from the Third World*, 383.

14. Chung Hyun Kyung, *Struggle to Be the Sun Again*, 72.

15. Mary John Mananzan, "The Filipino Woman: A Historical Perspective," in *Culture, Women, and Theology*, 50.

16. Ibid., 54.

17. Ibid., 56.

18. Ibid., 61.

19. Ibid., 64.

20. Virginia Fabella, "A Common Methodology for Diverse Christologies?" in *With Passion and Compassion*, 110.

21. Virginia Fabella, "Christology from an Asian Woman's Perspective," in *We Dare to Dream*, 111.

22. Ibid., 3.

23. Ibid., 5.

24. Kwok Pui-Lan, "Ecology and Christology," in *Feminist Theology*, no. 15 (Sheffield, Eng.: Sheffield Academic Press, 1997), 113–25.

25. Ibid., 116.

26. Ibid., 121.

27. Ibid., 124.

28. Aruna Gnanadason, "Women and Spirituality in Asia," in *Feminist Theology from the Third World*, 352–53.

29. Aruna Gnanadason, "Toward an Indian Feminist Theology," in *We Dare to Dream*, 71.

30. See Daphne Hampson, *After Christianity* (London: SCM, 1996).

31. Monica Melancton, "Christology and Women," in *We Dare to Dream*, 18.

32. Gabriele Dietrich, quoted in *Struggle to Be the Sun Again*, 66–70.

33. Ibid.

7. Liberating Power, Liberating Praxis

1. Both women challenged the received doctrines in significant ways— Margery entering the divine life through visions of equality with Christ, and Hildegard challenging male leadership. There are many examples of such women and men who told alternative tales based in liberative power.

2. See Hampson, *After Christianity*.

3. See Richard Gross, *Psychology: The Science of Mind and Behaviour* (London: Hodder and Stoughton, 1992), 401–587.

4. Carol Christ, *The Rebirth of the Goddess* (Reading, Mass.: Addison-Wesley, 1997), 44.

5. Heyward, *The Redemption of God*.

6. See Asphodel Long, *In a Chariot Drawn by Lions* (London: Women's Press, 1991).

7. See Isherwood and Stuart, *Introducing Body Theology.*

8. See, for example, Origen (185–254); Irenaeus (130–200); Athanasius (296–373).

9. Joan Casanas, quoted in Pablo Richard, *The Idols of Death and the God of Life* (New York: Orbis, 1982), 122.

10. The work of James Lovelock suggests that nature does not work on the principle of survival of the fittest but in a more symbiotic and harmonious way. See, for example, *Gaia: A New Look at Life on Earth* (Oxford: Oxford University Press, 1982) and *The Ages of Gaia* (Oxford: Oxford University Press, 1995).

INDEX

ACT UP, 103
African theology, 12, 39–44; and
    African Americans, 23–36; and
    women, 44–48
Ahn Sang Nim, 114, 157
alienation, 52, 53
Althaus-Reed, Marcella, 62, 154
Aquino, María Pilar, 64, 65, 154
Asian theology, 110–27

Beckford, Robert, 36, 37, 153
Bingemer, María Clara, 61, 62
black Messiahs, 44, 47
black theology, 22–35; in Britain,
    35–37
Boesak, Allan, 41, 153
Boff, Leonardo, 54, 55, 57, 154
Bojaji Idowu, E., 39
Brock, Rita, 80, 81, 85, 156
Brooten, Bernadette, 90, 156

Caribbean, 35–37
Chokmah, 74
Christ: black, 22, 25, 34, 117; erotic,
    93–102; of faith, 137–42; Filipino,
    118–22; guru, 124–27; of history,
    136–42; indecent, 63; liberating
    narrative, 130–32; organic, 122–24;

queer 102–6; relational, 76;
    web of liberation, 64–65
Christ, Carol, 139, 158
Christology of risk, 147–49
Christo-politics, 82–83
Chung Hyun Kyung, 112, 113, 115,
    116, 157, 158
Clark, Michael, 100, 157
Cleague, Albert, 26
colonization, 11, 13
colonizers, 38
Cone, James, 27–30, 41, 152
Congregation for the Doctrine of
    the Faith, 91
Council of Chalcedon, 49, 95
Countryman, William, 106, 157

Daly, Mary, 69, 70, 71, 85, 140, 141,
    147, 155
dependency theory, 8, 9
Dietrich, Gabriele, 127, 158
Douglas, Kelly Brown, 31, 33, 36,
    152
Dread, Jesus as, 35–37
Driver, Tom, 105
dunamis, 78, 97, 98, 99, 142

EATWOT, 11, 13, 58

ecofeminism, 123, 137
ecology, 76, 87
ekklesia of women, 84
erotic power, 80, 82, 145
exousia, 97

Fabella, Virginia, 121, 158
feminist theology, 57, 68–88

Gebara, Ivone, 60, 61, 65, 66, 154, 155
Gnanadason, Aruna, 123, 158
Goss, Robert, 91, 92, 156, 158
Grant, Jacquelyn, 31, 33, 152
Grey, Mary, 78, 80, 85, 155
Gutiérrez, Gustavo, 6, 52, 57, 58, 66, 151

Hampson, Daphne, 125, 138, 158
han-pu-ri, 112–14
hermeneutic meditation, 10
Heyward, Carter, 49, 50, 77, 78, 85, 93–102, 142, 145, 156, 157, 159
hypostatic union, 95, 112

inculturation, 39, 47
indigenous culture, 48
indigenous spirituality, 57, 58, 63, 64

Jesus: as Dread, 35–37; of history, 137–42; Jesus Seminar, 1; as unclean friend, 106–7
Johnson, Elizabeth, 86–87, 156

King, Martin Luther, 26, 41
kingdom: of God, 132–36; of mothers, 78
Kuan Yin, 117–18
Kwok Pui-Lan, 112, 122–23, 149, 157, 158
kyriarchy, 83–85

Lee Oo Chung, 116, 158
Logos, 74

Malcolm X, 26

Malleus Maleficarum, 71
Mananzan, Mary John, 118, 120, 158
Marx, Karl, 1, 9
Marxism, 7, 8, 9, 11, 42, 157
Marxists, 7, 8, 9, 11, 17, 42
Mary, mother of Jesus, 26, 114, 119
Mbiti, John, 39
Medellín Conference, 6, 8, 49
Melancton, Monica, 125, 158
Mesters, Carlos, 54
Mollenkott, Virginia, 94, 156
Moltmann-Wendell, Elisabeth, 76, 77, 78, 85, 155
Mosala, Itumeleng, 41

NAFTA agreement, 16
Nasimiyu-Wasike, Anne, 44, 45, 153
Nicene Creed, 4, 32, 49

Oduyoye, Mercy Amba, 43
Omega Point, 49, 67, 149
orthopraxis, 54
OutRage, 103

Park Soon Kyung, 117
power: of being, 69; of Christ, 145–47; of erotic connection, 146; of God, 131; in relation, 79
praxis, 18, 52; personal, 101; liberative 46; redemptive, 5
process thought, 57, 60, 69

queer Christ, 103–7
Queer Nation, 103
queer theology, 89–109

racism, 22–24
racist culture, 26
redemption: erotic, 80–82; praxis, 5
resurrection, 80, 82, 140, 146; power, 82; praxis, 140
Ritchie, Nelly, 63, 64
Rodriguez, Raquel, 60, 154
Ruether, Rosemary Radford, 57, 68, 70, 71, 72, 74–76, 81, 151, 154, 155
Russell, Letty, 74, 75

Schüssler Fiorenza, Elisabeth, 70, 72, 82–86, 147, 155, 156
Shakti, 123, 124
shamanism, 112, 117
Shekinah, 74
Shiva, Vandana, 123, 152
Sobrino, Jon, 49, 50, 53, 55, 56, 153, 154
Sophia, 83–87, 147
Sophialogy, 86
Stanton, Elizabeth Cady, 68, 85
Stonewall Riots, 102
Stringer, Martin, 108, 157

Suffering Servant, 45, 115, 134

Tamez, Elsa, 63, 154
Thomas, M. M., 41, 42
transgressive politics, 102, 103
Truth and Reconciliation Committee, 39
Tutu, Desmond, 41

Williams, Delores, 32–33, 152
Williams, Robert, 105, 157
womanist theology, 30–35